Heart Bar Ranch

And Johnson Valley Neighbors

By Martha Wood Coutant

Revised & Republished by the Morongo Basin Historical Society

Heart Bar Ranch
And Johnson Valley Neighbors

By Martha Wood Coutant

First Edition
Printed In 1985

-

Second Edition
Revised By Stanley O. Coutant & Printed In 1986

-

THIRD EDITION
Revised & Republished by the
Morongo Basin Historical Society in 2019

ISBN NUMBER: 978-1-64713-223-1

www.MBHS.net

First Edition

Acknowledgements

To Mynard Swarthout for making available the ledgers, papers, and journals of Albert J. Swarthout, the diary of Lillie Swarthout, and clippings from the San Bernardino Sun.
Also personal recollections as told to Willena Hansen.
Also to "Raising the Dust" by Julian Smith Gobar, and "Range One East" by Virginia C. Hemphill-Gobar.
And to Clarence E. Goodridge, Woodrow C. Shehorn, Kendall J. Stone, Esther Haddan, and Lee Berry for their memories and able assistance.
And appreciation to the Johnson Valley Journal editor Lorelea Hazard.

The Swarthout Family Tree

Donald Mynard Swarthout

Born	1899
Died	Feb 17th, 1980
Married	Jan 7th, 1928
Wife:	**Gailene F. Finley**
Born	July 3rd, 1896
Died	September 11th, 1982

Children:

Mynard F.	1929-2015
Elizabeth	1931-1976
Janet	1937-2008

Albert Riley K. Swarthout

Born	Feb 11th, 1872
Died	Nov 10th, 1963
Married	1895
Wife:	**Lillian Furstenfeld**
Born	Apr 26th, 1870
Died	July 26th, 1954

Children:

Helene	1896-1897
Donald M.	1899-1980

George W. Swarthout

Born	April 6th, 1817
Died	April, 1872
Married	June 5th, 1862
Wife:	**Elizabeth Jane Brain**
Born	Aug 10th, 1843
Died	Feb 2nd, 1922

Children:

Charity S.	1863-1954
Susannah	1864-1884
Phillip Charles	1867-1961
George Edward	1869-1946
Albert Riley K.	1872-1963

Phillip Swarthout

Born	1792
Died	- - - -
Married	1820
Wife:	**Charity Bates**
Born	May 4th, 1794
Died	March 17th, 1877

Children:

George W	1817-1872
Nathan M.	1823-1903
Harley	1831-1915

The Morongo Basin Historical Society is grateful to Stan Coutant for the opportunity to publish a new edition of Martha Wood Coutant's *Heart Bar Ranch and Johnson Valley Neighbors* in a revised format. Since 2003, the Historical Society has been holding annual events at Old Woman Springs, winter headquarters for Heart Bar Ranch operations. Martha Coutant was present for the Old Woman Springs dedication in 2004 when she signed copies of her book.

Over the years, the book has become indispensable to understanding an earlier era. Its rich description of cattle drives in the mountains, cowboy life, well digging, desert homesteading and more, brings history to life. Through it all is the story of the remarkable Albert Swarthout, cowboy, forest ranger, timber locator, and store manager. Swarthout initially homesteaded Old Woman Springs Ranch in 1907. First with partner Charlie Martin and later with J. Dale Gentry, Swarthout was part owner of Heart Bar Ranch for almost 40 years. It was "Swarty" who ran the cattle operations.

We had several goals we wanted to accomplish in bringing out a revised edition of *Heart Bar Ranch and Johnson Valley Neighbors* that we are hoping will appeal to and reach a wider audience. First, we wanted to organize most of the photographs, journals and account statements in appendices with accompanying explanations as needed. Next, we wanted to add photographs and documents that had never been included in any of the editions. Third, we wanted to publish the manuscript in book form with a redesigned cover. Finally, from the beginning, we knew we were not going to change one word of Martha Coutant's text.

Martha loved the desert, saying in the May, 1968 edition of The Desert Whispers, "Johnson Valley is the most beautiful spot in the desert." In the monthly newsletter which she published in the 1960s she reported on everyday life: pancake breakfasts, club meetings, and visits from friends and relatives. Eventually, after Martha and her family had been weekending in Johnson Valley for some years, she heard about the Heart Bar Ranch history and decided that it needed to be told along with stories about her homesteading Johnson Valley neighbors. She published her first edition in 1985.

A great many people have assisted us in publishing this revised edition. We are so thankful to Morgan Reche, son and grandson of two Heart Bar cow hands, Walter and Charlie Reche. Morgan's stories about his family and growing up are a direct link to the past. We have included several of his family photographs in our new edition. Another link to the past, Steve Kelley, nephew of Cathleen Kelley Raymond, grandniece of Albert Swarthout, was kind enough to send us the studio portraits of Albert and Helene. He also furnished the details and photos of Swarthout's and Gentry's final visit to the Heart Bar Ranch at Big Meadows in 1963.

We received expert help from Jennifer Dickerson of the San Bernardino County Museum, Sue Payne of the California Room at the San Bernardino Public Library, and the County of San Bernardino Historical Archives in finding newspaper articles and photographs of brands, the Heart Bar Ranch and the Swarthout family.

Morongo Basin Historical Society member Bill Wilson, formerly a resident of Johnson Valley and editor of the Johnson Valley Journal, donated quality copies of many of the photographs in the book. He also provided a copy of the 1974 letter written by Donald Swarthout to Bill Guldborg included here for the very first time.

Thanks to John and Barbara Marnell, authors of *Good Samaritans of Death Valley*, for supplying us with the interesting photo of Lou Wescott Beck and the road sign for Old Woman Springs. Steve Hanson, Site Chairman for the Morongo Basin Historical Society, provided expert help in developing the Swarthout family tree. Importantly, Steve has actually visited, documented and photographed many of the places mentioned in the book: Rattlesnake Spring, the Rock Corral, One Hole and Two Hole Springs, and Ames Well.

Bob Troyer, in Hawaii, helped improve the quality of many of the photos. We really appreciate the assistance and support from the Johnson Valley Improvement Association and the folks at the Lucerne Valley Market.

We especially thank Bert and Donna Barber for allowing the Morongo Basin Historical Society to hold annual tours at Old Woman Springs Ranch. Visiting the beautiful and unique ranch is an annual highlight for the Society and its guests.

We were so fortunate to have met Stan and Dixie Coutant, June, 2018, at Johnson Valley for the first time. They were immediately receptive to our proposal for the Historical Society to publish a new and updated version of *Heart Bar Ranch and Johnson Valley Neighbors*. Since then, their support and assistance have been invaluable. We cannot thank them enough for allowing us the opportunity to present Martha Coutant's wonderful history of people, events and life in earlier days.

Kenneth B. Gentry, Charlie Rossow, Claudia Spotts, James Spotts
Heart Bar Ranch and Johnson Valley Neighbors Book Committee

SWARTHOUTS AT BOX S. LEFT TO RIGHT ARE ALBERT, UNKNOWN WOMAN, HELENE AND LILLIE.

Born in Arlington, Massachusetts during 1913, my mother, Martha Wood, along with her five sisters and their parents, migrated west to California in 1926, where they landed in Pasadena. One of their first west-coast experiences was to buy an XLNT tamale, which they planned to share. Conditioned to a lifetime of New England boiled dinners, they found the spices in the tamale were so intense that between the eight of them they could not finish it.

Although born in San José, my dad Stanley Coutant and his family moved to Apple Valley while he was still quite young. He grew up there, and attended local schools.

After meeting and marrying in 1934, Martha and Stanley bought a house in Sierra Madre and moved in. I arrived nine years later.

One day in 1954 an announcement appeared in the *Los Angeles Times* describing five-acre parcels in California's high desert being offered by the Bureau of Land Management at $25 an acre. My dad reminisced about memories of the Victor Valley area, so a visit to the region was planned.

Our first trip was my initial experience with the Cajon Pass, the Mojave Desert, and concluded with what seemed to be a long journey on a dirt road. I learned this was "the county road" that connected Lucerne Valley to Yucca Valley. Back then it seemed barren. But we had arrived in Johnson Valley! I was eleven.

We homesteaded a five-acre parcel at the southern edge of Timico Acres. Most Friday evenings we jumped into my dad's 1948 Studebaker Commander towing a fifteen-foot long travel trailer, and made the 118-mile journey from Sierra Madre to Johnson Valley, only to return to town Sunday evenings. We were labeled "weekenders" from "down below" by the then-few permanent Johnson Valley residents.

During 1957 we hired a Yucca Valley-based contractor with the unique last name of Katje, pronounced "cagey," who built us a one-room cabin with an attached tank house.

Martha worked for the *Monrovia Daily News Post* as its Arcadia correspondent, and it was not long before she turned her news-gathering abilities to collecting local items of interest. During the sixties she published *The Desert Whispers of Johnson Valley*, a monthly mimeographed newsletter that was available via subscription. Eventually her coverage extended to Old Woman Springs, where she began hearing anecdotes about two old-time cattlemen named Dale Gentry and Albert Swarthout, partners in an endeavor to raise cows in the Big Bear area during the summer months, driving them to Old Woman Springs and Rock Corral for wintering.

Martha's research resulted in the publication of *Heart Bar Ranch and Johnson Valley Neighbors*, the book you are holding, first printed in 1985, with subsequent reprints during the intervening years.

—Stan Coutant
Tehachapi, California
February, 2019

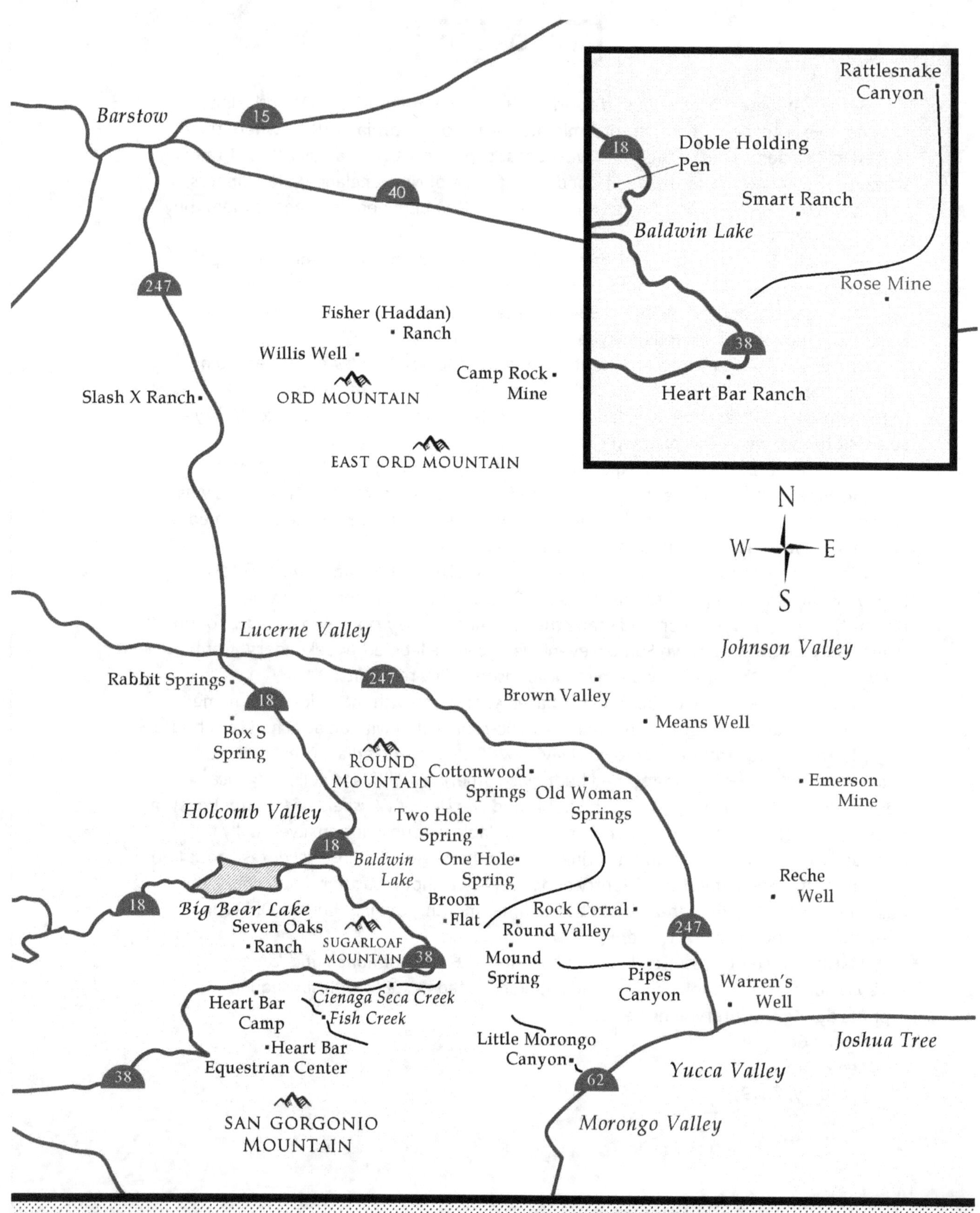

SAN BERNARDINO COUNTY

TABLE OF CONTENTS

Branding livestock to designate ownership was practiced in California as far back as the sixteenth century and began within what is now San Bernardino County in the late eighteenth century. Prior to 1917 in California, a livestock owner's brand was recorded by each county.

The San Bernardino County Recorder would examine burned imprints from the branding irons brought in by livestock owners and would record them in the *San Bernardino County Brand Book*.

Most of the imprints submitted to the county were made on small square sections of leather. But some cattlemen brought in brands made on anything that they had available, such as wood boards or leather strips removed from old furniture or luggage.

On November 18th, 1853, James W. Waters became the first person to have his brand recorded in San Bernardino County and a total of 790 brands were recorded in the *San Bernardino County Brand Book* from 1853 until 1917.

Some registered brands were actually the result of broken branding irons or other errors. James Smart first registered the "IS" brand which was later acquired by the Talmadge brothers. Smart meant to register the brand as "JS". But before he could have the brand recorded, the curved part of the "J" was broken off the iron, turning the brand into "IS" instead of "JS". Opting not to repair or replace the branding iron, Smart simply registered it in its damaged condition.

This page and many others within this book contain examples of the various cattle brands which have been used in San Bernardino County. The Talmadge "IS" brand appears on page 30 and is illustrated to show the missing portion of the original "J" turned into an "I".

HEART BAR RANCH BRAND

BEGINNINGS

In 1907 Albert Swarthout homesteaded Old Woman Springs in Johnson Valley.

Swarthout first homesteaded in Lucerne Valley about 1893, establishing the Box S Ranch, where he built a cabin and dug a well. He was about 21 years old at that time.

The Box S was a mile from Rabbit Springs. The closest neighbor was Peter Davidson, a Scotsman, the first man to homestead in the area in 1877. Davidson established a way station where teamsters and their mule teams stopped for food and water on the way to and from the many mines in the area. Davidson was a cantankerous old fellow who did not get along with everyone. But Swarthout and Davidson established a lasting friendship. Well-driller Julian Gobar stated that Swarthout was shrewd, with a good sense of humor, who was able to get along with everyone.

"He was a tease," Gobar said.

Swarthout soon determined there was not enough natural feed for grazing cattle at Box S. He planned on a substantial herd, and began a search for the ranch of his dreams.

He was carrying on the tradition of his pioneering ancestors.

Philip and Charity Bates Swarthout were married in Utica, New York, about 1820. They had seven children: George, Nathan, Harley, Charles, Truman, Hamilton and Lucinda. The family moved with western expansion of the country, going to Ohio, then to Kansas, and on to Utah. Philip worked in Salt Lake City on construction of the Mormon Church.

His son Nathan was a soldier, and was with General Kearney on the march from Leavenworth to Los Angeles during the Mexican War in 1847. He was sent to San Bernardino with a detachment to put down an Indian uprising. Nathan wrote to his relatives in Utah, sending glowing accounts of the beauties of San Bernardino Valley.

Swarthouts were on the move again. In 1851 they joined a wagon train captained by Andrew Lytle coming from Salt Lake City to San Bernardino.

George, Nathan and Harley established adjoining ranches, extending from Little Mountain almost to Base Line. They built cabins in the mountains, but soon abandoned them because of trouble with the Indians and marauding bears. They bought grazing land in what came to be known as Swarthout Canyon, now Wrightwood, began operating cattle ranches, and helped build a fort where the courthouse now stands.

The brothers did not rush into marriage. Nathan was 28 when he married 20-year-old Emma Tanner in 1851, soon after she arrived in San Bernardino by wagon train.

George was 45, an established rancher, when he returned to Utah to marry Elizabeth, 19 years old, who had been born in Bath, England.

Harley was 38 when he claimed Mary Lytle as his bride in 1869. She was 20 years old, born in San Bernardino a year after Andrew Lytle led the first wagon train over the Mormon Trail.

The three brothers fathered seventeen children, and soon had a crop of home-grown ranch hands. George's brand was 2 and a backward S, recorded in 1855. Hamilton's brand was HS. A diamond with a tail at the bottom was recorded by Harley in 1880, possibly Diamond J.

Albert R. Swarthout was the youngest of five children born to George and Elizabeth. He was born in San Bernardino on Feb. 11, 1872. His father died two months later at age 55.

When Albert left his Box S Ranch, he supervised wood-cutting in the mountains and supplied fuel for the trains traveling through Cajon Pass. This was a short-lived business as the railroad soon turned to burning oil.

In Hesperia Swarthout met Lillie Furstenfeld. They were married on Feb. 10, 1895, at the home of the bride's parents in Alhambra.

Swarthout was a cattleman, "first, last, and always," he said. But he needed time to locate good grazing land. He got a job with the U.S. Forest Service, and was the first ranger in charge of the area from Cajon Pass to Lake Arrowhead. He also marked timber for the stamp mill at Rose Mine. From 1899 to 1905 he patrolled for the U.S. Forest Service. A small journal of "field notes" records his daily routine from June through September in 1905.

On Thursday, June 1, he writes, "Was packing and storing household goods." On Friday he "left E. Highland at 4:20 a.m. with team for summer camp at Seven Oaks. Arrived at 4 p.m., 30 miles." Saturday he unpacked and fixed up around camp. He began his rounds at 8 a.m. Sunday, posting 16 fire notices along the trail from Converse Flat to Snyder's, and was back at camp by 4:30 p.m., a trip of 16 miles.

He worked all day Monday on Bear Valley Trail, cutting brush and filling in. He covered 14 to 20 miles a day, posting fire notices at camp grounds and cabins. He built a corral in the horse pasture near the cabin, and worked on the road from the cabin down to the river.

There is no mention of his wife Lillie, who apparently stayed in San Bernardino. A letter from her Uncle Joe in Peachland was posted to her on Feb. 6, 1900 at 556 Union Ave, in San Bernardino.

The letter congratulates her on the birth of a son and heir. The writer hopes "the boy will at least partially fill the void and dissipate some of the sorrow caused by the loss of your dear little girl. I sincerely hope that you may live to see him grow to manhood." Son Donald did live to manhood and provided his parents with three grandchildren.

The writer also refers to Christmas "when I had to play the accompaniment to Old Nick as I used to when you thought, or was made to believe he came down the chimney at night to fill your stocking." There was a phone in the cabin at Seven Oaks, but Swarthout mentions only one call, which regarded a fire.

His Field Notes, General Land Office, tend strictly to business. His pay was $50 a month, and from that he provided his own provisions, and feed for two horses. The horses served as a wagon team, for riding the trail, and as pack animals. He posted ten notices on the 20-mile patrol to Big Meadows.

On Friday, July 6 Swarthout hitched up the team and at 5 a.m. left for San Bernardino, arriving at 4 p.m. He had the horses shod, bought provisions, and started back at 8 a.m. Saturday. No mention of visiting Lillie and five-year-old Donald. He stopped overnight at Camp 4 in Santa Ana Canyon, rose at 4 a.m., arriving at camp at 10 a.m. Sunday. He was barely unloaded when he got word of a fire. He loaded a pack horse and was off to the fire where he remained until, on Monday, "was all around the fire line, found fire safe," and was back in camp at 4 p.m.

In 1957, a controversy erupted regarding the best method for fighting forest fires. Swarthout was interviewed as a "retired San Bernardino cattleman and one of the first forest rangers."

Swarthout came down hard on fighting fire with fire, favoring controlled burning. He advocated cleaning out dense stands of brush which provide fast-burning fuel in disastrous blazes. The "San Bernardino Sun" noted that Swarthout, "now 85, stands straight as a young pine, and his bright, blue eyes light up as he speaks of ridges and canyons he knows as well as any man alive."

"Mother Nature turned these mountains over to us, and she has done a better job of managing them than we ever have," Swarthout said. He outlined a plan for clearing areas and staggering burns. "There are at least 50 places I can take you to where the brush is piled up as high as the ceiling of this living room — so thick a bird can't fly through it.

"In the old days, lightning caused most fires, usually a bolt hitting a snag top. I can remember when we had five going at once. However, this lightning was normally accompanied by rain, which held down the fire. Even so, we would let patches burn. In the winter, we would clear buffer lanes and do light burning in sections. The brush would come back in three years or so. We didn't let it get too heavy, like now, when the brush can create fires big enough to cause extensive damage and burn timber. As a result, we did not have many dangerous fires, although we had few men to fight them."

In the journal, Swarthout records his routine, checking fences, posting notices, clearing brush. Seldom did it vary. He returned to camp early one day, because of rain, but was back out in a couple of hours. Once in a while he met another ranger on the trail.

On Sept. 13, he had returned to camp when he saw smoke. He phoned to Redlands and was informed that the fire was in Richie Canyon. On Sept. 25, he again went to San Bernardino for provisions, and this time records staying overnight at E. Highlands. But no mention of family.

The journal ends on the last day of September.

Meanwhile, back at the ranch in Lucerne Valley, a squatter had moved in on Box S. James "Dad" Goulding, who later became a pillar of society in Lucerne Valley, took up residence in 1897. Swarthout relinquished his claim to Goulding, who developed a very successful operation. He brought in a fancy new contraption called a rotary drill, and drilled a well, bringing in a steady flow of water, a big event at the time.

In 1904, it was discovered that poor old "Uncle Pete" Davidson had been living on the wrong land for 30 years. He had filed for land on Range One East, but had proved up on land on Range One West. A Los Angeles Deputy Sheriff discovered the mistake and contested the homestead. The case went to court. Swarthout put up the money to fight the suit. The lower court ruled in favor of the deputy. Swarthout provided more money to take the case to a higher court. This time the court ruled in Uncle Pete's favor. Too late. Uncle Pete was gone. He had died at the way station on Jan. 7, 1906, before the decision was handed down.

When Swarty left the forest service, he walked the flume for a year for Pacific Power and Light. The next year he spent in Otis, now Yermo, managing a store, hotel, and post office for a brother. Lillie helped.

On November 18, 1907, Swarthout purchased a half-interest in the Heart Bar Ranch in Big Meadows, south of Big Bear Lake, from R. F. Garner. The price was $915. The sale included 37 head of stock cattle branded Heart Bar, a bay Arizona horse, and two old wagons. Also range privileges in the forest reserve commonly called Big Meadows, South Fork, and other ranges in the Santa Ana canyons. Included were range privileges on the desert side of the mountains northeast of Big Meadows, commonly called Rock Corral, One Hole Spring, Two Hole Spring, Clear Springs and Quail Springs. Garner retained one-half interest in "sixteen head of aged Arizona steers," to be cared for and sold without expense to Garner. Charlie Martin owned the other half of Heart Bar.

The Heart Bar brand was first recorded on January 14, 1884, by Martin and Button, and was signed by W. F. Holcomb, county recorder. The cattle ranged in the mountains during the summer. In the fall they were moved to the desert in three herds. The third group was moved after the first snowfall, when the cattle came out of the mountains to Big Meadows and could be rounded up.

On the desert side, range privileges extended from Lucerne Valley on the west to Pipes Wash on the east, and across the valley for ten miles. Shacks were built, some stone, some wood, where provisions were stored. Beans, coffee, flour, meal, and side meat were tied in bags and hung from the rafters to keep from animals. Cats were kept at each station to keep the rodent population down. Stations were at Old Woman Springs, Ames Well, Rock Corral, Cottonwood and Rabbit Springs.

In the same year that Swarthout bought into Heart Bar, he homesteaded Old Woman Springs. In 1856 a surveying party found several elderly Indian women living at the springs and gave it the official name of Old Woman Springs, the name that has appeared on maps since 1857.

The Swarthouts found many metates while working the ground at the ranch. The ranch house was ringed with Indian relics which disappeared over the years. At one time the Johnson Valley area was called "the Dry Lakes Mining District." At least forty gold mines were worked in the district, W. C. Shehorn noted.

Gold was $20 an ounce when Emerson took out about $50,000 worth at Emerson Mine, before he was asphyxiated by a gas-powered generator at the bottom of the shaft. Maurice Donahue found the body, he said. Another story says that Emerson's partner was overcome by fumes. Emerson went down to help him, and both suffered the same fate.

When Martin and Swarthout began their partnership, there were four small buildings at Big Meadows: two cabins connected by a breezeway, a cabin with a fireplace, and a blacksmith shop.

Swarthout moved a one-room cabin from South Fork for the family's first home at Heart Bar. Donald was seven years old. The Swarthout's first child, Helene, died of appendicitis at three years of age. A large photo shows a beautiful child with blonde pigtails in a long, lace-trimmed yellow dress. Donald remembered taking a bath in the one-room cabin and feeling the wind blow through the chinks. Swarthout boarded up the chinks which made a nice runway for mice.

A rattlesnake made its home under the breezeway. One day the snake crawled out and settled down to sun itself next to Swarthout's feet. Swarty decided he was a good mouser and deserved to live. And he did, for quite some time.

The first cookstove was brought to Heart Bar by Martin and Swarthout. They borrowed the biggest mare available at Harvey's Pack Station, and loaded her with a stove and a tripod. The mare packed the stove for thirty minutes, then was stopped to rest for thirty minutes. The tripod was set up, and the stove was hung from it. Alternating periods of packing and resting were continued for the entire trip. The group arrived at Heart Bar very late that night.

MARTIN CATTLE BRAND

CHARLIE MARTIN

Charles Martin was Al Swarthout's first partner at Heart Bar Ranch. Charlie was hard, tough, and weighed about 200 pounds. Violating a law did not bother him. His motto was, "If anyone does you dirt, do him ten times worse." Well driller Julian Gobar remembered Charlie as "cold and hard, to be treated with care."

According to local history recorded by Willena Hansen, Charlie killed a man in a San Bernardino bar shoot-out, apparently in self-defense, following a verbal argument. His opponent missed — several times. Charlie did not.

In 1884 Charlie and John Denney were arrested and charged with assault with intent to commit robbery. Denney was sentenced to state prison for eight years. Charlie was found guilty on a reduced charge, and was sentenced to county jail for one day.

In 1889 Charlie was arrested for arson and perjury, but the charges were dropped. In 1900 he was arrested for possession of illegal deer, and the charges were dismissed.

Charlie ran a pack train of burros, two strings, and kept them moving constantly between the mountains and San Bernardino. Big as he was, he used a burro as a cow pony and rode it hard. He named it Grover Cleveland, after the president. Charlie was of the opinion that "Cleve" was as tough as he was.

In 1873 Charlie and two partners staked a mining claim near 29 Palms. Charlie suffered from what he called "exclamatory rheumatism" from working in damp mines. At one time he was laid up, suffering, when his partners discovered a Frenchman had jumped their claim. When Charlie was sufficiently recovered, the partners let Charlie go to the mine without telling him what he would find.

Charlie left his gunbelt in the buckboard at the top of the hill and walked down to the mine. He met the Frenchman and accusations flew. The Frenchman drew a knife and began slashing Charlie. Charlie knocked him down, and retreated a few steps up the hill. Again and again the Frenchman attacked, and Charlie knocked him down and retreated a few steps. When he reached the buckboard, he grabbed his gun and — still holstered — killed the claim jumper. Charlie was tried for murder, but was acquitted when he removed his shirt in the courtroom, revealing over 40 stab wounds in his arms and chest.

In 1887 Charlie homesteaded Glen Martin, now Camp Angelus. The area became known as Mountain Home, especially to Charlie's many invited guests. He built a larger house, and made it into a resort for his friends. The settlement around Igo's in Mill Creek is still called Mountain Home. The first white settlers at Big Meadows were two Mormon families. They lived there two years, then discovered they were on the wrong fork of the Santa Ana River. They resettled at Seven Oaks, leaving in 1857 or 1858 when recalled to Salt Lake City by Brigham Young.

Bert Coomb was the next settler at Big Meadows, followed by William and James McHaney in 1890. Dudley and Dewar became owners of record in 1893, although they had been using the pasture in the 1880s. Dudley and Dewar sold to Connie Mack and Charles Martin. It is not certain just when Martin had approached a rancher named Button for a loan to go into the cattle business. Button decided he'd rather go into partnership with Charlie than loan him money.

On January 14, 1884 the Heart Bar brand was recorded in San Bernardino by Martin and Button, the same year Charlie spent a day in the county jail in July.

Hardy Lord said he hired on as a butcher for Martin and Button in 1904. Just where they ran their cattle is not clear, nor what became of Button. Connie Mack and Martin went into partnership at Heart Bar in 1893, and Martin kept the Heart Bar brand. Possibly Charlie had many irons in the fire at all times. Connie Mack sold his interest to R. F. Gamer, who sold to

Albert Swarthout in 1907, and Martin and Swarthout were in business at Big Meadows and Old Woman Springs.

Charlie and Swarty spent the better part of a winter developing water at Rock Corral, 12 miles east of Old Woman Springs. They dug two tunnels into the mountain and piped the water to a trough in the corral. They lived in a shack equipped with a stove, two beds, chairs and a table while working on the water. Later Charlie went to Rock Corral for a routine check and found the stove was missing. He followed wagon tracks to a shack. The stove was inside. No one was around.

Charlie lived by his motto. He returned to Old Woman Springs, hitched a team to a hay rack, and with several ranch hands returned to the homesteader's shack. The men loaded the building on the hay rack, and moved it to Mound Springs where it served as a trail shack for many years.

"It's against the law to break and enter, so I took the whole shack," Charlie explained. The homesteader made a brief inquiry, then wisely faded into the sunset.

Charlie had a son and a daughter, but the boy had died young. Charlie took Donald Swarthout under his wing, and treated him like a son, taking him on hunting trips and on the trail. Donald was about nine years old when he and Charlie went to a celebration in San Bernardino where confetti throwing was the chief occupation of the day. Don threw a handful at a confetti vendor, who objected and spoke out.

Don recalled that Charlie "picked one off the sidewalk and hit the fellow on the chin." The vendor's derby hat flew off, he landed on his back, the confetti tray perched on his stomach. Charlie took Don's hand and they walked away.

Charlie's daughter Myrtle married Cliff Shay. The Shays lived on the family homestead at Camp Angelus, and took care of Charlie's wife Julia, who was mentally ill. Cliff kept the books for Charlie's business interests. At one time, Charlie owned the land now occupied by Patton State Hospital. He traded it for land in Yucaipa. He also owned a gold mine, "The Tin Can," located at the mouth of Seco Creek. The mine was not profitable, but Charlie remedied that. He salted the mine and sold it to some gullible Englishmen.

When Charlie needed meat, he went out and shot it. A neighbor, Anthony Lewis, nicknamed "Anthy," once reported Charlie for having illegal deer meat. The meat was confiscated by the law and Charlie was fined $25. Charlie bided his time. The next time he saw Anthy leaning on his gate, he challenged him. Anthy said he did not have his gun. Charlie told him to get it. When Anthy returned with his gun, Charlie took it away from him and slapped his face. He then returned the gun, turned his back, walked to his horse, and rode away.

In 1914 Charlie sold his half-interest in Heart Bar Ranch to Dr. E. Scott Blair. After a long bout with cancer, Charlie died on March 7, 1927. Cliff Shay inherited the homestead at Camp Angelus when all of the Martins were gone.

Although some dates may be a bit confused, there is no doubt that Charlie Martin was one tough hombre, a man to be treated carefully.

WM. SHAY CATTLE BRAND

WIND & WATER

Old Woman Springs was winter headquarters for Heart Bar Ranch. Summer camp was in the mountains at Big Meadows. Range privileges on the desert extended from Lucerne Valley on the west to Pipes Wash on the east, in a strip about ten miles wide. The cattle watered at Old Woman Springs, Ames Well, Cottonwood Springs, Rock Corral, and Rabbit Springs, as well as other natural water holes. Usually the cowhands maintained the watering places. But in 1916 a problem arose at Ames Well. Quicksand plugged the well. Lack of water required that the cattle be moved to another well, and a cowboy was needed to keep the cattle from returning to their accustomed — and waterless — area. This was costly. Time was important.

Al Swarthout hired Julian Gobar, a young well driller from Lucerne Valley, to take care of the problem. "It was more or less in the nature of a gamble," Junie said. The problem was new to him, but he would try. Swarthout outlined the procedure and supervised the move to the well. Vern Stafford and Gus Yeager loaded the bedrolls and camping gear, and took a horse and its feed to a cabin about half a mile north of the windmill at Ames Well.

Swarty and Junie loaded the pickup with tools, grub, and water. Sherm Yeager, Gus' brother, was cook at Old Woman Springs. He cooked up a batch of doughnuts, a huge rice pudding, and a jar of beans. The four established the camp. Gus left to check for problems at Rock Corral, Swarty to tend well number five, north of Ames. Junie and Vern were left to do the job.

They rigged up a cable, pulley, and bucket to haul the sand out of the well. The horse pulled the heavy bucket to the surface. For two days they worked, making no headway. The sand poured in as fast as they dug it out. The last bucket load came up hard as cement. More water was needed.

Swarty arrived in the Model T with an apple pie from Sherm, to Junie's delight. In later years, Junie showed the results of his joy in eating.

Vern was needed to work with the cattle, Swarty said. The problem was discussed. A large volume of water was required, and the best way to get it would be to sink a shaft away from the present well to avoid a cave-in. More tools were needed, and someone to help Junie. Swarty and Vern headed for Old Woman Springs. Junie went on to Box Springs for tools and to see if Paul Hoak was available to work.

That was the night of January 27, 1916. The night of the Big Wind.

The wind was blowing so hard that Junie had trouble getting the horses into the shed at Rabbit Springs. He was concerned about his neighbors, two women and two children. Junie walked and crawled to the Millbanke shack. It was empty. He staggered, crawled, and walked toward a light, and found the group huddled on the ground. When he picked up one child to carry it, Mrs. Millbanke beat him with her fists. Nellie Gibbs picked up the other child and the four started off. Mrs. Millbanke came to her senses, picked up the lantern, and came after them. It was raining, and began to sleet. They walked, fell, and crawled. Boards and shingles were flying around from a neighboring shack, but they made it to Junie's cabin.

The wind was also creating havoc on the McNany homestead in Brown Valley, five miles north of Old Woman Springs. Mrs. McNany, 57 years old, lived on the homestead with her ten-year-old grandson, Max Sherwood, while her husband and sons worked in Los Angeles.

A loaded lumber wagon started to move down the hill, pushed by the wind. Mrs. McNany ran outside to stop it. She was struck on the head by a plank blown off the chicken coop, and died instantly. Max tried to get his grandmother to the cabin, but was unable to move her. He covered her with a blanket weighted down with stones, then crawled into bed with his cat and dog to wait out the storm.

The next morning was clear, cold, and calm. Max saddled up his pony, and rode to Old Woman Springs. Vern and Gus were the only ones at the ranch. They gave Max breakfast, then saddled up their horses, and rode out to the homestead, then into Lucerne to send a telegram to the family. When Junie and Paul Hoak went back to Ames Well, it was arranged that Max would stay with them to help, and to recover from an experience that was quite a lot for a ten-year-old.

Junie and Paul took turns digging a four-foot-square shaft, and were down twelve feet at the end of the first day. They averaged eleven feet a day. Evenings they sat outside, and watched the moon come up over the Bullion Mountains. They listened to the coyotes howl. In the silence, they heard the coyotes running along the edge of the dry lake, their claws kicking up sand and pebbles. They told stories to entertain Max, and hoped it helped him to recover from his experience.

On the fifth day, the cable broke and the bucket fell to the bottom. Paul was looking up, saw it coming, and moved out of the way, a great relief to Junie.

The next day water began collecting in puddles at the bottom of the shaft. More lumber was needed to make a tunnel to the well under the windmill. Back at Old Woman Springs, Gus was delegated to drive the team to Victorville to get the lumber. Max's parents were at the ranch. They were through with the desert. They took Max as he was, torn clothes, needing a bath, and drove away, leaving the desert for good.

While waiting for the lumber to arrive, Junie and Gus took care of the watering holes in Johnson Valley. The first day, they took the team and buckboard to Mesquite Well, six miles from the ranch. The wind had pulled the derrick of the windmill out of plumb. Using a tackle, they pulled it back in line, tightened bolts, replaced leathers and valve facings, and changed the oil.

The next day they went to Rattlesnake Canyon, where they fixed a hole in the pipe with a strip of inner tube and bailing wire, then on to Two Hole Spring, where the only problem was a broken fence wire. At One Hole Spring, everything was in order. The following day they rode to Means Well to clean out the runway trough. Swarty had tried to maintain a windmill to pump water at Means Well, but changing winds twisted the tower, wrecked the wheels, and kept blowing the tail off. Water was sixteen feet down.

Swarty had remedied the situation by scraping a runway down to water, installing a trough in the water where the cattle could drink, then walk up the runway on the other side. The only maintenance required was cleaning out the runway and trough once a year. The job was accomplished with a Fresno scraper, shovels, and large buckets. The last job was putting patches on the tank at Mesquite Well.

Back at the ranch, they found a wagonload of redwood for curbing the shaft at Ames Well. Gus and Junie set off with the team and wagon. It was slow going, but Junie enjoyed the scenery. Gus was in an unusual, talkative mood, and told stories of his days as cattleman, mining man, and stage driver. Junie considered it a treat.

Late in the day they reached Emerson Mine, unloaded the grub, and took the lumber to the well site. Gus returned to Old Woman Springs, and Junie started work while waiting for Swarty and Paul. The next day, a visitor arrived in a touring car. It was Paul Ames, owner of the cabin, out checking his mining properties. He brought with him a good supply of pork, bread, and fruit, which he shared with Junie. During the night a large packrat knocked down the dishpan, a big sound in the stillness of the desert. Junie savored every moment. Ames left in the morning, and when Junie went into the cabin to fix his lunch, he found that Ames had left all of his food for Junie, much to his delight.

When Paul and Swarty arrived, work began. A Windlass was rigged to lower sections of curbing into the shaft. It was slow work. Only eight feet of curb was lowered the first day. The next day they started digging, water came up, and was soon two feet deep.

A pump was needed. Swarty went to the ranch, soon returning with an engine and pump jack. It took four days of hard work to set the curb. The construction began on a complicated arrangement for shoring up the tunnel. It was Junie's first experience with tunneling and timbering. When the tunnel was five feet high and three wide, the sand caved in. A more complicated method of timbering was required.

Junie records every move in detail in "Raising the Dust," making up timbers, driving wedges, driving in planks. Water came in as fast as it was pumped out. The men worked in their underwear. They kept their shoes on because they had to use their feet to press the timbers in place.

The last two days they worked in water up to their armpits. When the job was finished, Swarty hoisted the men up. He met them at the top with blankets to wrap up in. Paul and Junie were jubilant. A difficult job was accomplished. The shaft and tunnel would enable the cylinder to deliver its average flow without unduly agitating the quicksand. Junie asked Swarty if he would consider the money well spent if the well worked for twenty years. Swarty said he would. Forty years later, in 1956, Ames Well was still producing, much to Junie's satisfaction.

JULIAN GOBAR REPAIRED AMES WELL, 1916.

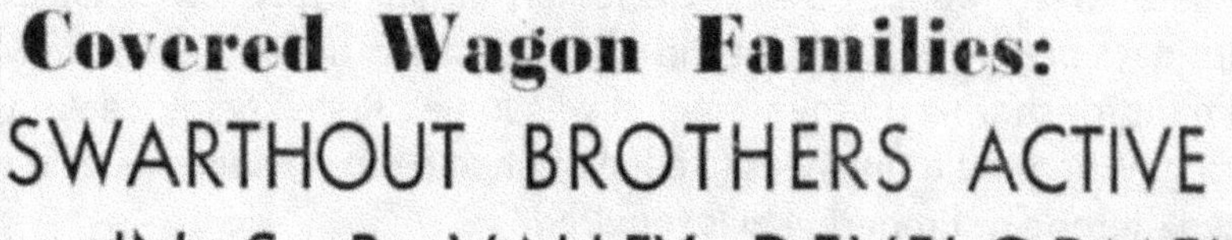

Covered Wagon Families:
SWARTHOUT BROTHERS ACTIVE IN S. B. VALLEY DEVELOPMENT

First of Clan Came To California As Soldier

Swarthout, George W., born in Utica, N. Y., April 6, 1817, and Elizabeth Jane Brain, born in Bath, Eng., Aug. 10, 1843, married at Provo, Utah, June 5, 1862.

Swarthout, Nathan, born in Norwalk, Ohio, Aug. 16, 1823, and Emma Tanner, born in Kirkland, Ohio, June 1, 1831, married at Sycamore Grove, Aug. 25, 1851.

Swarthout, Harley, born in New London, Ohio, Feb. 1, 1831, and Mary Lytle, born at San Bernardino, July 30, 1852, married in San Bernardino, July 7, 1869.

Headed by three brothers, George W., Nathan and Harley, the Swarthout family played an important part in the development of San Bernardino valley.

The first Swarthout to reach California was in San Bernardino in 1847—four years in advance of the colonists from Salt Lake City. He

Above, at left, George W. and Elizabeth Brain Swarthout; right, Nathan and Emma Tanner Swarthout, and, below, Harley and Mary Lytle Swarthout. The Swarthout brothers were among the early settlers of the valley.

THE TUESDAY, DECEMBER 20TH, 1938 EDITION OF THE SAN BERNARDINO SUN. (CONTINUED ON PAGE 12)

THE YEAGER BROTHERS

Gus and Sherm Yeager were brothers who worked at Old Woman Springs prior to 1920. The brothers were in their seventies, and very spry when he became acquainted with them, Junie Gobar said. Sherm was the cook, and an excellent one. But he went on sprees and disappeared for days at a time. Gus, Swarty or Verne would take on the cooking duty in Sherm's absence. When Sherm returned, he moved back into his routine. Swarty never mentioned the interim.

Gus was a teetotaler, but he also had times when he wished to get away from it all. He packed up and walked to Rose Mine to stay with the caretaker, Al Watts, for a month or two.

Swarty also welcomed him back without comment.

One cold winter day Gus left Rose Mine, telling Al he was heading for Baldwin Lake. It snowed that day. At Old Woman Springs it was presumed that Gus was at Rose Mine. Al Watts figured he had returned to the ranch.

Gus never showed up.

Sometime later Buck Haddon was out looking for Heart Bar cattle in Cactus Flat and found the remains of Gus. He buried him where he found him.

Junie ran into Sherm on the street in San Bernardino. Sherm told Junie the doctors said he had tuberculosis. Sherm knew it was not TB, just "consumption." He was an outpatient at the sanitarium. Sherm begged Junie to get up a posse and find Gus. He was sure he was holed up somewhere in a remote canyon. Sherm had made one trip looking for his brother, but the snow had been four feet deep and he abandoned the search. Junie made inquiries and was told of Buck's grim find. He wrote to Sherm at the sanitarium but never received an answer, and thought that Sherm might have joined Gus before he got word. The Yeager brothers were well-liked and were treated with tolerant affection by all who knew them, Junie remembered.

ROSE MINE TOWN AND THE STAMP MILL IN THE EARLY 1900's.

Covered Wagon Families:
SWARTHOUT BROTHERS ACTIVE IN S. B. VALLEY DEVELOPMENT

(Continued from Page Eleven)

was Nathan Swarthout, a soldier with General Kearney on the march from Leavenworth to Los Angeles during the Mexican war. He came to San Bernardino with a detachment of troops to put down an Indian uprising. He was at Sacramento when the announcement of the discovery of gold was made.

OTHERS FOLLOW

The glowing description of San Bernardino valley by Nathan Swarthout to other members of the family, who in the meantime had migrated from Leavenworth to Utah, caused various Swarthouts to join the wagon train captained by Andrew Lytle from Salt Lake City to San Bernardino in 1851.

The Swarthout family group included Philip and Charity Bates Swarthout, who had married at Utica, New York, about 1820, and seven children: George W., Nathan, Harley, Charles, Truman, Hamilton and Lucinda.

wife of John Dean; Rolland Swarthout, wife Ruth Sturges. They are the children of Harley M. and Minnie Swarthout.

Tibby Hammond Forsythe, wife of R. D. Forsythe, San Bernardino. She is the daughter of Cyrena Swarthout Dunbar.

Howard Swarthout. He is the son of Harry and Eva Swarthout.

FOURTH GENERATION

James K. Guthrie, wife Margaret Gallagher; Kathleen Guthrie. They are the children of Mr. and Mrs. James A. Guthrie.

Stephen F. Kelley; Kathleen Kelley. They are the children of Mr. and Mrs. James F. Kelley.

Harold J. Swarthout, Robert W. Swarthout of Grandview, Wash. They are the children of Mr. and Mrs. Walter L. Swarthout.

Patricia Ann Schoenberg, Mary Jane Schoenberg, Merna May Schoenberg of Chewelah, Wash.

They are the children of Mr. and Mrs. Robert L. Schoenberg.

Fay Irene Blackburn, Hermosa Beach. She is the daughter of Mr. and Mrs. Fay R. Blackburn.

Patricia June Bark, Georgia Mae Bark, Lawrence A. Bark Jr., of Manhattan Beach. They are the children of Mr. and Mrs. Lawrence A. Bark.

Mynard Swarthout, Elizabeth Swarthout, Janet Swarthout of Altadena. They are the children of Mr. and Mrs. Donald Swarthout.

Audrey Swarthout Yermer, wife of Frank Yermer; Randall Swarthout, Doris Swarthout, Patricia Swarthout, of Hemet. They are the children of Mr. and Mrs. Ernest Swarthout.

Douglas Swarthout. He is the son of Mr. and Mrs. Howard Swarthout.

Jeri Forsythe. She is the daughter of Mr. and Mrs. R. D. Forsythe.

Athlyn Swarthout. She is the daughter of Mr. and Mrs. Rolland Swarthout.

(CONTINUED FROM PAGE 10)

FROM THE LATE 1800S-1900S, CATTLE WERE DRIVEN THROUGH RATTLESNAKE CANYON UP TO BIG MEADOWS FOR SUMMER GRAZING & BACK TO THE DESERT FOR THE WINTER.

CATTLE DRIVES

Cattle driving on Heart Bar Ranch cannot be compared to the long, hard drives on the big Texas ranches, which often took a month or more. But three days in the mountains is a microcosm of a long drive. Canyons were narrow, crowding the cattle. The animals slipped on the rocks, wore down their hooves, and dodged into bushes to hide. Calves strayed from their mothers, and cows lagged behind, looking for their calves, all bawling mournfully. Bad weather, stampedes, and long days did not make life easier.

In May or June, the cattle were moved up through Rattlesnake Canyon to Big Meadows. There they ranged through the mountains and canyons. Summer thunderstorms kept the pasture growing, and five or six were anticipated each year. As fall approached, two or three hundred head were herded into Big Meadows, where a buyer selected his beef. Heart Bar cowboys moved the cattle down the south side of the mountain.

On the north side, twelve acres of desert land were kept in alfalfa at Old Woman Springs. Once a month during the summer, a crew came down from the cool of the mountains to harvest the alfalfa. They had to work fast in the heat, because high temperatures could cause the alfalfa to shatter. Pitching was done by hand from shocks to a wagon to a galvanized iron barn which stood in the sun. Cooking was done on a wood-burning stove in a 12-by-12 shack, which was worse than pitching hay in the sun.

At the end of summer, before the cattle were brought down, cowboys went to the desert to clean out the wells and water holes, and repair windmills. When the weather cooled, the drive to the desert began. The trail was up Cienaga Seco Creek, over the divide, down Arrastra Creek, through Broom Flats, to the corral at Round Valley. There a tiny shack contained a stove, and a table and stools which were moved outside to make room for bedrolls after the evening meal.

The second day's drive was down Rattlesnake Canyon to Mound Springs, where Charlie Martin's portable shack and a corral awaited. The third day's drive was to the desert floor, where the cattle were turned loose to roam at will. The men returned to Big Meadows for the second bunch. When the first snow fell, and the cattle and deer came down out of the canyons looking for food, two or three men would ride from Old Woman Springs to bring down the last of the herd.

Donald Swarthout recalled some winter rides without any desire to return to the old days. The horses were shod with special shoes to get a foothold on the ice: a steel bar in the toe, and the heels turned down and sharpened. A crew left Old Woman Springs while the stars were shining. Two burros carried grub and blankets. The men traded the job of breaking trail as the snow was often chest-deep on the horses. At times it was necessary to dismount and leave the horses. Wet snow clung to the men's clothes, and they often arrived at Big Meadows in frozen clothing.

The burros and horses were taken care of first. An iron plate and tin can were removed from the chimneys of the cabin before a meal could be cooked and frozen clothing dried out.

Early the next morning, the search for the cattle began. Many could be found near Sugarloaf, under the big trees. Because of the shortage of feed, it was necessary to round up the herd and start down the hill within four days at the most. Every head had to be accounted for.

One year, against all the ranch rules, Don Swarthout went to the mountains alone. Charlie Reche was supposed to go along, but he had to make an unscheduled trip to the dentist. All went well, and Don was rounding up a small herd, which included one angry two-year-old steer. The steer ran into the willows. Don dismounted and went in on foot. The steer charged. Don backed up, caught his foot on a branch, and fell on his back. The steer continued to charge. Don drew his .38, and shot the animal at the base of a horn, stunning it. Don retreated. The next morning, the steer was docile, and easily led to the meadows.

Don recalled a roundup when two 15-year-old boys joined in, happy to be real cowboys on a cattle drive. They were Dr. E. Scott Blair's son and his friend Hippo. Charlie Reche was camp cook. The first night he cooked steaks. Hippo complained his was too rare. Charlie said nothing.

The next day they crossed the ridge to Little Morongo, where they found a dozen unbranded cattle, including a three-year-old bull and several yearlings. The cattle stampeded. The men gave chase, and so did Hippo's horse. The horse took Hippo through every clump of brush in the canyon. When the cattle were stopped, Hippo emerged from the brush, still on his horse, but scratched, bleeding, and crying. Wiping his eyes on his sleeve, he said, "If I get out of this alive, I will never be a cowboy again."

By the time the cattle were calm and could be moved, it was moonlight. They reached camp at 1:30 am. Charlie built a fire and began cooking. He handed a frying pan and a wooden stake to Hippo, saying, "Here, Hippo! Cook your own steak."

It was not Hippo's finest day.

It was expected that some cattle would be found dead on the range every year. One or two were lost each year in Fish Creek. Swarty made every effort to treat every injured or sick cow. But some years were disastrous. The cattle seemed to be dying of poison. There was larkspur growing at South Fork, but the cowboys pulled up every plant they could find. A lethal dose for a cow is about 30 pounds, and the cowboys were sure there were not two pounds left in the area. Dr. Blair performed an autopsy on a cow, and sent the findings to U. C. Davis, but no conclusion was reached. Swarty observed that mushrooms always popped up in profusion after a thundershower. He thought that might be the cause of the poisoning, but the facts were never determined.

During the winter of 1938-39, a heavy, warm rain fell on four feet of snow. The meadows became a sheet of water. The creek was washed out in one afternoon, causing a tremendous drop in the water table. The meadow dried up, and the lush green never returned. These were among the crushing blows that led to the end of Heart Bar ranching.

Heart Bar cattle were sold to buyers who came to Big Meadows in the fall. Heart Bar cowboys were responsible for getting the cattle down the mountain to the buyer.

The earliest beef drives were made down Santa Ana Canyon to a field west of Glass' in Section 17, where they stopped for the night. The second day cattle were driven by Camp Weesha, to a natural corral formed by the mountains. Here the road became so rough and narrow that only 20 head could be taken through at a time. On Heart Bar there was a milk cow named Bawly that could be led with a rope tied around her horns.

The cattle were divided into cuts of 18 to 20 head. Swarthout led Bawly, setting the pace, followed by two cowboys driving the first cut. A hand drove the second cut, another the third, and so on, until all of the cattle were moving through the canyon.

Two cowboys rode drag, which required extra skill. They watched for signs that any cattle had broken away, then tracked them down and returned them to the herd. Some cattlemen were able to look at their herd and know instantly if any were missing.

On the third day, the cattle were driven into San Bernardino. Later, when John Garner was the buyer, the herd was moved on to Riverside on a road that paralleled the railroad, then on a bridge that crossed the tracks.

On one drive, the engineer blew the whistle as the train neared the herd. The cattle stampeded into an orange grove which was being irrigated, and bogged down in the mire. Charlie Martin was riding drag. He agreed with the owner that there was considerable damage, but said the cattle belonged to John Garner, although technically not true until delivered. Garner was not pleased when approached for damages, but gave the grove owner a quarter of beef, which was acceptable.

During one drive to San Bernardino, Swarty experienced his closest brush with death. The cattle had been grazing in the cool mountain air at South Fork. They had to be moved before the first killing frost, or the feed would decline and the cattle would lose weight. It was still hot in San Bernardino in late September. As they neared the lowland, a big bull became overheated, lay down, and refused to budge. Swarty hit him with a rope. The bull did not move. Swarty dismounted, picked up a syrup can from the ground, and threw it at the bull, which was facing away from him. The can hit one of its horns. The bull leaped up. Swarty ran to his horse, but did not make it.

The bull's horns caught Swarty by the legs, and lifted him onto its head, then tossed him aside and charged a burro that was tied to a tree, disemboweling it. It continued charging, broke through a fence, and finally halted in a pasture holding a dairy herd.

Swarty escaped with only bruised ribs. The bull was left in the pasture overnight. The cowboys returned before daylight, just as the dairy owner was coming to get his herd. The remarks are not recorded, but it is said that 75 per cent of cowboy language consists of strong words. The bull was driven to a loading pen, where it remained until a truck and driver arrived to chauffeur it in comfort to the stockyard.

In 1914, loading pens were built between Mentone and East Highlands. A control road was constructed between Camp Angelus and Seven Oaks. Twelve acres were fenced at Harvey's Pack Station, where cattle could be corraled overnight. The drive was made easier.

An alternative route was attempted for a short while, but proved worse than the first one. The cattle were driven from Heart Bar to Big Bear Valley, and held in a corral that belonged to Bill Shay, just north of Baldwin Lake. The second day they were driven down Cushenberry Grade to the Box S, and held in a field until nightfall. In the cool of a moonlit night, they were driven into Victorville, to be shipped by train. But the drive was hard on men and cattle, and was discontinued.

The last drives were made on the most successful route, down Mission Creek, across the Indian reservation to Whitewater, where the cattle were loaded onto trains. Only one overnight stop was required, and hay and oats for the horses were stored at the camp. Eventually a road was built to South Fork, and the ranch hands continued it on to Heart Bar. The cattle were then trucked out. Most of that road has since been washed out.

The cattle always lost weight on the drives. Swarty had scales built at Heart Bar. The cattle were weighed, the buyer paid, subtracting an estimated loss of four per cent on the drive. But Heart Bar men still did the driving. When the cattle were reweighed in Los Angeles, the loss was usually closer to eight per cent.

In 1914 Charlie Martin sold his half-interest in the Heart Bar to Dr. Blair. In 1918 Swarthout sold his interest to Bob Bryant. There are hints that Bryant and Blair did not get along. Dr. Blair purchased Bryant's interest about 1920. He was sole owner for only a short while. In 1921 Dr. Blair, his wife and son were killed when their car was struck by a train in Hesperia.

In the settlement of the Blair estate, Swarthout and his new partner, J. Dale Gentry, purchased Heart Bar Ranch. On April 11, Swarty was back on familiar ground.

Gentry was a San Bernardino businessman, who owned a hotel and other property. Swarthout was still a cattleman, through and through, a point he emphasized on occasion. The purchase included 600 head of stock cattle, and 179 bull calves and heifers for $35,000. In addition, 250 feeder steers were bought for $7,171. The partnership lasted almost twenty years. According to the ledger presented to the court during litigation, there were 1,029 head of cattle grazing in Johnson Valley in 1922. The business broke even the first year, with cost of operation slightly over $12,000, and sale of cattle almost $13,000.

Among those on the payroll were Warren Reche, D. H. Richardson, Tom Pierce, Buck Haddon, and Walter Reche. The going rate for cowboys was $40 a month and board. In 1924, profits rose to $2,000, and in 1925 the books show $6,000 net. The cowboy's pay was raised to $50 in 1926, a good year, when the ranch netted $10,000.

A letter from Swarthout to Nash Boulder, Forest Supervisor, dated December 29, 1925, was an answer to an inquiry regarding the Heart Bar leased land. "Have twenty sections leased in the forest reserve 12,000 acres," he wrote. He lists the sections. "Rental charge $233.91. Running between 500 and 600 head stock cattle during grazing season, April 1 to November 1. Losses about two per cent while on leased land. Steers sold net weight 936 pounds at $5.60 per hundred FOB cars. Extra cost three men at $50 per month and board equal to $75 per month per man for seven months total $1,575. Cost per head for grazing 550 head for $233.90 — 42 1/2 cents per head per year, .0355 per month."

In 1929, the year of The Crash, no cattle were sold. Expenses were $4,812, and two hundred head of cattle were found dead. In 1930, sales were $6,000, but expenses were $9,000, and 50 head died. Things were tough everywhere. The Swarthouts borrowed money from Mrs. Swarthout's mother, Mrs. Furstenfeld. In 1932, there were 689 head on hand, and of these, 158 were found dead. A slight profit was realized in 1935, although 50 head died.

Cost of trucking cattle was $3 a head, and cowboys were working for $25 a month. Gasoline was 16.5 cents per gallon. Frank Critzer put in 40 hours at the ranch for 30 cents an hour. Critzer led a strange life at Giant Rock. No one knew for sure what he was up to. In 1942, federal agents went to the rock to investigate. Critzer set off an explosion, killing himself. The agents escaped uninjured.

Willie Boy, the object of the last manhunt in the area, also worked for Swarty. During the chase, Willie Boy went to Old Woman Springs, but no one was there. Swarty said later he felt that had he been there, he might have talked Willie Boy into surrendering without bloodshed. Charlie Reche was shot during the chase, and walked with a limp for the rest of his life.

WATERING TROUGH AT RATTLESNAKE CANYON ON THE MAIN TRAIL TO AND FROM BIG MEADOWS.

ED GROHS

When Ed Grohs was 17 years old, he went to work for Albert Swarthout. Ed rode for Heart Bar for two years, in what may be the best and the worst years for the ranch.

In 1932, at the age of 12, Ed quit school to go into the cattle business for himself. He and his brothers, George and Charles, often bought horses from Swarty. Ed was 17 and the owner of 23 head of cattle when he received a letter from Swarty with the offer of a job. Working for Heart Bar was Ed's longtime dream. He sold his cattle and signed on. He went to work on the desert under the tutelage of Clay, a six-foot-seven cowboy from Arizona. Ed worked through the winter and in the spring roundup, and had started at Big Meadows when Clay was fired. Clay had a habit of overstaying his trips to town."

Swarty warned Ed, "This country is pretty, very pleasing. But don't enjoy it so much you don't take care of my cattle." Ed started work at $25 a month, and was soon raised to $35.

The drive from Broom Flats was particularly rough, Ed said, because the hills were steep and covered with shale. It took hard driving to coax the cattle into Round Valley. The cows were tired by the time they had climbed to the top of Rattlesnake Canyon. The spring drive was even more difficult because of the new calves. Sometimes a cowboy would carry a new calf, but usually the cow and calf were cut out and left to come in on their own. A cow and calf can become quite frantic when separated. Ed believed that cows and calves have their own code — "Always return to the last place we saw each other."

It was not always possible to keep all the cattle in sight in Cienaga Seco, because of the mountain mahogany and brush, and the men had to track the cattle. Bulls would be the first to tire, because they are heavy and slow, and often were left behind, especially when they started to fight. Ed has seen bulls fight for hours, until after sundown. "They cannot be stopped," he said.

The Talmadge brothers also ran cattle on the desert, and often made the drive with Heart Bar. Just below Rose Mine, the herds were split, Talmadge crossing over into Bear Valley, and Heart Bar into Round Valley. If any cattle were mixed up, they were sold, and the owner received the payment. Cyanide was used in the gold-extracting process at Rose Mine, which poisoned the water. Cattle died from the bad water until the mining company was forced to fence the property.

The year 1936 had been slow, the ranch barely breaking even, with only 90 head sold, leaving a balance of 636 head to start the new year.

Sales were brisk in 1937. Cattle were sold every month. But 286 head were found dead. In spite of the loss, sales totaled over $18,000. Expenses were $5,000, which included a payroll of $2,329. Beef was selling at six to eight cents a pound on the hoof.

The depression was still around. Problems arose. Swarthout and his partner, Dale Gentry, were disagreeing. No cattle were bought in 1938. The payroll was cut in half. Only four hands were kept on full time, including Ed, Charles Knox, W. Wright and Howard Whipple. Extra hands were hired when needed.

That winter, the rains came. It was a disaster all over Southern California. Houses were washed out, damage was widespread. At Heart Bar, a warm rain fell on four feet of snow, and the meadows became a lake. A huge gully appeared in one afternoon. The washout caused a tremendous drop in the water table. The meadow that had been a lush green every summer dried up. Sale of cattle and two horses brought only $797. The loss that year was $2,015.

GENTRY'S LODGE AT BIG MEADOWS.

SWARTY & GENTRY ATTEND A BARBECUE AT BIG MEADOWS IN 1925.

THE LAST ROUNDUP

Howard Whipple and Ed went out to drive in the last few head. Howard had come from Arizona to work at Heart Bar in 1932. After three years, he returned to Arizona, but was soon back on the payroll at Heart Bar.

Most of the remaining cattle were up Cienaga Seco. In the canyon, Ed and Howard jumped two steers, which immediately ran and disappeared. The cowboys tracked the steers over the ridge to Big Bear, and back. The tracks came to the place where the cattle were first sighted, then dropped down the Pipes and toward the desert. There was blood in the tracks, a sign that the shells of their hooves were wearing down. That afternoon, Ed and Howard caught up with the steers, which immediately hushed up in the scrub.

The men were tired and annoyed, or they would not have launched into an episode lasting for hours, that must have resembled a Marx Brothers ruckus: in and out of the brush, taunting the steers, trying to get a rope on them, and coming close to being trampled. When the steers were finally roped and secured to a tree, men and beasts were angry.

Howard and Ed returned to Seco, where they found a yearling, and in the bright moonlight, captured it and tied it to a tree. It was 2:30 am. when they reached Heart Bar. They reported to Swarty, and it was decided to truck the cattle back.

The saga continued. Ed and Howard found the big steer lying down. They sawed six inches off its horns so that it could not harm the horse. When the animal got up, it immediately attacked Howard's mount, then fled to the scrub and hushed up. Another scramble. Eventually the steer was roped, and led a mile to the waiting truck, retreating to every bush along the way. The small steer appeared calm, but every time it was almost in the truck, it would lie down and slide out. After three hours of this, the men buried the back end of the truck, and the steer was dragged in.

Back at the ranch, Swarty inspected the animals. He decided the kindest thing was to let them go. The small steer went to the creek, drank, foundered, and died. The big steer walked to the water on its knees. For about a month, the steer walked on its knees until its feet were healed. Every other day its horns were treated because of maggots.

It was the last roundup for Swarty. Ed always regretted the fiasco. The payroll dropped to $949 in 1939. In 1940, the payroll was $537, and the loss $950. Ed took the horses down to Old Woman Springs, and for a while broke colts for Swarty. But without cattle, it was not ranching as far as Ed was concerned, and he quit. The ranch went into receivership.

Ed went back into the business for himself, and managed a successful operation for many years. He leased a ranch in Victorville, where he ran 1,100 head. He also operated a ranch in Covina, grazing about 300 head at Sugarloaf in the winter. "Perseverance and patience covers all of the cattle business," Ed said in retrospect.

HEART BAR RANCH SALES & EXPENSES FOR SELECTED YEARS							
	1922	1927	1928	1929	1937	1938	1940
Cattle Sales	14,214.25	9,054.12	8,025.99	0	18,479.99	797.76	
Expenses	12,000.00	6,224.93	5,256.82	4,812.00	5,159.26	2,812.85	950.00
# Sold	207	104	80	0	310	0	0

HEART BAR RANCH HAND WALTER RECHE ON BAMBOO WITH HIS DOG BUTCH BY GOAT MOUNTAIN.

1928		
Apr. 26 @ $2.50 per day	Apr 28 Check	$6.25
and brand 2 1/2 days $6.25		
May 9 @ 40.00 per mo		
Apr 28 2 1/2 days @ 2.50	6.25	
May 14 @ 40.00 per mo	10.00	
June 15	30.00	
July 10	Hay Cutting Expense	
July 17	40.00	
Aug 14	40.00	
Sept 7	40.00	
Oct 14	40.00	
Nov 1 Check in full	30.60	
	236.85	

1929		
Apr 17 4 day @ 3.00	12.00 Apr 22 Check $12.00	
" 22 @ 40.00 per mo		
May 3 Check	13.30	
May 31 "	40.00	
June 14	22.65 In Full	
Dec 16 Check	25.00 Dec 1 Began Work	
" 28	20.00 In Full	
	132.95	

WALTER RECHE'S PAY DETAILS FROM 1928 & 1929.

LILLIE

Lillie Furstenfeld and Albert Swarthout were married in 1895. Lillie was the daughter of Martin and Elizabeth Furstenfeld. Her father was a German immigrant. Lillie was born in Vallejo. The family moved to Santa Ana, then to Hesperia, where Lillie met her future husband. Mr. Furstenfeld was a businessman, and apparently a good one, for in 1931, during the depression, Mrs. Furstenfeld loaned the Swarthouts $1,500 at six per cent interest. A second loan of $500 was made in 1932, and a third for $1,500 in 1933. The debt was repaid in regular monthly installments.

Albert was managing a store for one of his brothers when he met Lillie. The Swarthouts soon moved to San Bernardino, where their first child was born in 1896. The little girl died of appendicitis before her second birthday.

Fifty years later, Lillie began a diary on January 1. Her first thought is of her daughter, writing: "Helene, 26 January, 1896 — passed 1897." Son Donald was born in 1899, when Swarty was working as a ranger in the San Bernardino mountains. The Swarthouts maintained a home in San Bernardino all through the years when Swarty was a ranger or running Heart Bar Ranch.

Lillie played piano, and for a while augmented the family coffers by holding dances in the San Bernardino house. Couples paid 50 cents admission for dancing and refreshments while Lillie played piano. Donald Swarthout grew up in San Bernardino and on Heart Bar. He expected to take over operation of the ranch. He attended Redlands High School and Pomona College, and in 1922 was graduated from Oregon State.

In 1922, there were 1,029 Heart Bar cattle grazing in Johnson Valley. But coming events were casting shadows. Grazing land was shrinking as people moved into the valley. The Swarthouts could see that Heart Bar Ranch could not be a profitable operation for many more years. Donald agreed that he should look in another direction. He took postgraduate work at Iowa State College, and joined the faculty there. But in a short while, he returned to California to work for the California Walnut Growers' Association.

A crumbling newspaper clipping announces a wedding following "a happy romance amid the pines and glorious scenery of the San Bernardino heights." Donald Swarthout claimed as his bride "Miss Gailene Finley, a lovely and accomplished young woman, daughter of Col. and Mrs. S. H. Finley." Col. Finley was on the board of supervisors of Orange County. The bride was a graduate of Monmouth College and Bryn Mawr, and "had traveled extensively in Europe." The gift from the bride's parents was a "beautiful motor car" in which the couple departed on a wedding journey.

When Lillie began her diary in 1946, Donald and Gailene were living in Altadena, and Lillie had three grandchildren, Mynard, Janet, and Elizabeth.

In 1940, Gentry wanted to dissolve the partnership and sell the ranch. Swarty asked the court for a division of the property. The matter was in litigation.

Lillie gives a daily report of events at the ranch, the last year they were to spend at Old Woman Springs, although they did not know it at the time.

The diary continues on January 1, "Son Donald and family left for home." The Swarthouts were preparing for a trip. On the third, they left in the rain for San Bernardino. On the fourth, they started back up through Cajon Pass at 5:30 a.m. in the rain and onto a windy desert. They made 330 miles that day, and camped outside Merced for the night. In Merced they attended two funerals and assisted one widow in settling her affairs. A telegram was received telling of the death of yet another relative. They shopped and visited in Vallejo and San Francisco.

On the twenty-sixth, the Swarthouts headed for home, buying ten gallons of gas in Merced for $2.35. By the thirtieth, they were back on the ranch, and the next day, "Dad raked and burned leaves." Almost every entry begins with "Dad." Dad irrigated, pruned trees, caught gophers, went for cattle, and checked wells and water holes. Cattle were moved, trucked, treated, and fed. Cattle was the business of the day.

While the case was in litigation, Heart Bar was put in the hands of a receiver, and was leased to Joe Denny and H. B. Ward. Swarty stayed on at the request of Denny and Ward.

Lillie was never lonely. Day after day, she notes the comings and goings of Denny and Ward, of visitors, hired hands, and friends. Don and family came out often. Swarty was 74 years old at the time, and put in a good day's work, even when "Dad was not so well." While picking pears, he fell from a ladder, but the next day was out "working on the ladder."

Mynard and Janet were at the ranch whenever possible. Mynard recalls pleasant times. As a teenager, he thought life on a ranch with the cowboys was the best of all possible worlds. He was 17 the last year at Old Woman Springs, driving the truck, herding cattle, and helping in the ranch chores. He remembers the silence, and the sound of a tree branch, heavy with water, crashing to the ground with a thunderous roar.

Lillie wrote, "A new man came — Sid." Sid Smith, Mynard recalls. Day after day, Dad and Sid checked wells, went up canyons for cattle to Means Well, and to Rock Corral. Ward and Denny came out, alone or with their families. Sid's family came often to visit. Junie Gobar, well driller, was a frequent visitor.

"Plenty company," Lillie writes.

The wind blew in March, and cattle were moved up Rattlesnake Canyon, or to Arrastra, or to Rock Corral. Dad, Sid, and Ward worked on the tunnel at Rock Corral. Dad sawed wood, cleaned the furnace, shod his horse Rowdy. A coyote got a guinea hen in April.

The men worked on a stove,"got gas in okay," [possibly butane] and "I cooked dinner all fine." Janet's ninth birthday was observed on April 14. On April 26, everyone attended the funeral of Dr. Gobar, Junie's father.

Cowboy Ed Grohs recalled that "Mrs. Swarty had her own way of keeping the hands in line." If around the night campfire the stories became too rough in her opinion, she would say, "You know, a cowboy is only a sheepherder with his brains knocked out." Buck Haddon recalled that the coffee at Old Woman Springs was terrible. Mynard recalls it was all a wonderful time.

Lillie and Swarty made frequent trips to San Bernardino. Scheduled court hearings were repeatedly postponed. Lillie mentioned the first strawberry. There were many fruit trees on the ranch, and Swarty irrigated the old orchard and the new orchard. Mynard remembers eating the fruit: magnificent, juicy pears, peaches, apples, cherries, and figs. Everyone helped picked fruit in season, and Lillie canned. When fishing season opened, Dad and Don went to the Sierras, returning in a few days with one good-sized fish.

In the middle of May, all hands turned to preparations for the move to Big Meadows. Cattle were moved to Rattlesnake Canyon. Sid trucked a load up through Big Bear to the meadows. Denny brought more cattle in a truck. The birds were getting after the apricots.

On the twenty-third, Ward arrived with a cook, and "plenty of grub." Ed and George Grohs started moving the cattle. On the twenty-fourth, all hands rode. Two men rounded up cattle at Rock Corral and Mesquite. The next day they made it to Round Springs. Sid and the cook returned for the balance of the stuff. Don trucked horses to Big Meadows and returned for another load

Lillie and Swarty remained at Old Woman Springs all that summer. Dad irrigated, took care of the water holes, and rounded up the remaining cattle.

They drove to San Bernardino and voted on June 4.

Lillie canned figs and peaches. Swarty fixed a leak at Rock Corral. Company still arrived even in the summer heat. Lillie put them to work peeling fruit. The September hearing was postponed. In October the cattle were started down from the mountains. Swarty went up to meet them. In November the hearing was again postponed. Swarty shod Rowdy, irrigated, fixed fences, moved cattle, and took hay to cattle. A coyote snagged a hen in November. Work was started on building a cabin in December. On Christmas day, "Big time, big feed. Ham," Lillie wrote in big letters. Don and family were there. Don left for home at 3 am. Gailene and the three children stayed on. The temperature was 22 degrees. The tomatoes and all the pipes froze. Swarty and Mynard checked wells and water holes to make sure the cattle could get water.

Dad "did not feel so good," but he went on working, moving cattle to Silver Reef, to Barrel Springs, and to Rock Corral. "Too cold," Lillie wrote.

In February, "Gentry and two fat men arrived, and took notes all over." Swarty went to San Bernardino to see his lawyer, Will Guthrie. The irrigating went on and on. Lillie and Swarty went to San Bernardino, where Dad went to the dentist and Lillie went to a foot doctor, who discovered that two bones in her foot were out of place.

On March 16, Gentry and his lawyer were at the ranch. The next day, Swarty conferred with Guthrie. On March 18, 1947, all were in court, and the matter was settled. "Property divided. All settled but signing," was all that Lillie wrote in her diary.

A newspaper clipping tells more. "The referees allocated the Big Meadows acreage to Mr. Gentry, and the desert land to Mr. Swarthout. Protesting that this division was unfair, Mr. Gentry said Mr. Swarthout was getting the best deal, and that the referees were biased and prejudiced. Mr. Swarthout declared he believed the referees to be fair, and he was satisfied with the division, and that he would take the part the referees had recommended for allocation to Mr. Gentry. The stipulated judgment dividing the property that way was then granted."

For a month the work went on as usual at Old Woman Springs. On May 12, Gentry sent a truckload of his belongings to Old Woman Springs. On May 21, Lillie and Swarty began packing. Forty years after he had homesteaded at the Springs, Swarty was leaving for good. Don helped in taking the tank, an icebox, "a big load," to Big Meadows. On May 23, Lillie noted, "Dad and I to mountains."

In the mountains, the work went on, shoeing horses, moving cattle, building a chicken pen, mowing the lawn, and again, "Plenty company." On August 4, Gentry arrived, and took two loads. On Sunday he "Gave Dad the key." The next day, two more loads were moved, and on the twelfth, Gentry took the last of his belongings.

Lillie's only comment was, "All hope G. never comes back." Lillie continued the diary for the rest of the year. Sid stayed on at Big Meadows, and Ward continued to visit. There was thick, cold fog, and on October 12, the first snow fell. Dad, Mynard, and Ward went looking for cattle in heavy snow.

Will Guthrie, Swarthout's attorney through long years of litigation, died on November 3. Lillie and Swarty attended the funeral on a cold, windy day. "A wonderful sermon," Lillie wrote.

On a trip to San Bernardino, Lillie counted 54 deer on the way down, and 51 on the return trip. They spent the day in town having new wills made.

The last entry in the journal is dated December 1. "Dad and Nick sawed wood, 11 a.m. snow."

After the division by the court, part of the land was deeded to Don and his family. In 1952, Section 20 was sold to the Blackwell Corporation. The Swarthouts moved to their San Bernardino home. Lillie died at the age of 84. Swarty remarried. He died on November 10, 1963, at the age of 91.

In 1956, the Blackwells lost the ranch to their lawyer, Harold Slain.

In 1964, the California Department of Parks and Recreation gained control of Heart Bar, and Heart Bar State Park was created. All of the old buildings were torn down. A 100-site campground was established, as well as a horse camp and a group camp. About 40,000 persons visited Heart Bar in 1975-76. The beaver were a big attraction.

Albert Swarthout's grandchildren, Mynard, Janet, and Elizabeth, spent vacations from school and many weekends at Heart Bar Ranch. It was a fabulous life for a teenager, Mynard said. On a ranch, riding horses, doing chores, being a cowboy. He was 17 years old the last year the Swarthouts spent at Old Woman Springs.

He remembers the fruit trees, the juicy pears, peaches, apricots, and figs. Everyone worked. His grandmother cooked, using desert sage for seasoning; she canned and raised chickens and turkeys. Mynard's father and mother dug a ditch by hand for concrete pipe.

Mynard remembers the sound of tree limbs, leaves heavy with water, crashing to the ground. a horrendous sound in the still desert air. And the clashing of horns when two bulls fought for hours.

He heard stories. When his father and grandfather hauled sheets of galvanized iron by horse and wagon to Mesquite Well. The Swarthouts riveted the large water tank, grandpa on the outside, dad on the inside.

Grandpa, working on the gearbox on top of the windmill. A sudden gust of wind, and grandpa grabbing for a handhold, smashing his fingers in the gears.

A Fordson tractor was kept running all night to pump water into the two reservoirs, to be run onto the alfalfa during the day. Swarty slept lightly, waking instantly when the tractor stopped, to run out and replace spark plugs.

After the ranch was divided, and Gentry was sole owner of Old Woman Springs, he brought a train from Hawaii. Gentry had worked on a pineapple ranch, and always hankered for one of the small trains used on the plantations. He imported ten miles of narrow gauge, and built a roundhouse. A steam engine pulled the tender, two flatcars, boxcar, and a caboose.

The train is gone. The ranch hands have scattered. Homesteaders have moved in, and a hiker may come upon a few scattered bones and abandoned water holes. Some of the ranch hands stayed in the area when Old Woman Springs ceased to be operated as a cattle ranch.

The Reches were early settlers, and worked at Old Woman Springs occasionally. Lewis N. James homesteaded in Johnson Valley northeast of the ranch on what is now Shehorn Ranch. James was in the junk business in Victorville when Woodrow C. Shehorn purchased the place in 1946. Prospectors in the Dry Lakes' Mining District frequented the James place because it had a windmill and water. "Woodie" Shehorn found many marked claims and considerable mining equipment when he moved in. Charles Ellenburg and his wife had lived in the shack for several years.

Jess Blair moved into Victorville where he ran a filling station and an auto repair shop. Buck Haddan bought a ranch in North Valley, and in 1939, at the ripe old age of 45, married Esther and settled down.

The Wilsons had a place in the valley. Their son Dale ran a gas station and repair shop in Lucerne Valley. He told stories of the tough times during the depression, and how everyone moved to town to be close to the welfare office. No one could afford twelve cents a gallon for gas to travel between Johnson Valley and Victorville.

The Swarthout years at Old Woman Springs spanned almost half a century, from horse-drawn wagons to paved highways and landing strips, and covered two world wars, the Roaring Twenties, and a depression.

From Highway 247, Old Woman Springs looks much as it did when operating as a cattle ranch, and anyone with memories and imagination can pretend that it still does.

BARKER CATTLE BRAND

BUCK HADDAN

Buck Haddan was born Robert Wesley Haddan in Stonewall, Colorado. Very early an uncle gave him the nickname of Buck, probably of necessity, for Buck learned to ride as soon as he could walk, wearing frilly dresses and sporting curls to his shoulders. The long coils mothers make by wrapping the hair around the finger.

By the time Buck was about six, he was graduated from dresses to a velvet Little Lord Fauntleroy suit, and shirt with white, lacy collar, still a handsome little chap with beautiful long curls.

Buck's father was a rancher. The family moved to New Mexico, where Dad managed the Adams Cattle Ranch, later the Bartlett Ranch.

Buck — minus the curls — moved on to Arizona, and rode for Phelps-Dodge until he decided he had seen enough cattle.

He moved to California in the summer, and joined a well-digging crew at Salton. That lasted three sweltering days. The green mountains beckoned, and Buck headed north, landing at Seven Oaks, near Big Bear Lake. He worked for a dude ranch. There he met Albert Swarthout ranching at Big Meadows, and Buck was back chasing cattle in the mountains in the summer, and in Johnson Valley in the winter.

But Buck could not settle down. He moved on down the hill to the Kellogg Arabian Horse Ranch in Pomona, and was back in skirts again, astride a horse. The riders dressed in the flowing "dishdasha" and headbands, traditionally worn by Arabs. This was during the twenties, when Pomona was the place to go on a Sunday afternoon to the Arabian Horse Show at Kellogg Ranch.

After Rudolph Valentino died in 1926, Buck rode Valentino's horse in the shows, and according to the photographs probably made feminine hearts go pitter-patter. He also rode in the Tournament of Roses parades. The Kellogg entry was a dashing group, controlling their spirited steeds with silver-ornamented saddles and flowing robes, prancing down Colorado Boulevard.

After a few years as an Arabian sheik, Buck returned to the desert and began putting a herd together. There he met Esther Crawford, a city girl from Los Angeles, who was visiting her brother's ranch in Lucerne Valley. Buck's wandering days were over. They were married in September 1939. For about a year, they ran cattle in North Valley. But people were moving in, crowding the cattle out. Buck and Esther moved farther out near Ord Mountain. For a while they lived in a miner's cabin on grazing land, then moved the cabin onto their own property. They improved and enlarged the building, and dug a well.

They operated the ranch through good times and bad, but always were able to make a living while many cattle ranches folded. They lived simply, far from neighbors, and were content. Evenings were often spent reading. Esther acquired the luxury of a gasoline-powered washing machine. When Buck rounded up his cattle, Esther drove the truck with equipment and feed. The cattle ranged across the valley to Willis Well, where Esther communed in spirit with Mrs. Willis.

Mildred Willis and her crippled husband lived at the well from 1915 to 1925. There Mildred began to work on her dream of a stone house surrounded by flower gardens. She was a small woman. Her husband built her a cart for hauling rocks. Mildred built a stone wall 660 feet long, four feet high, and almost as wide across the base of the hill to keep cattle out. She built rock corrals and pens. On a slight rise, she built what appears to be the foundation for her dream house. Walls in the wash apparently were to direct the water away from the house. It has been estimated that Mildred moved 1,372,000 pounds of stone. From the house site, one looks across the valley to the Haddan Ranch. Part way across, great spires of rock stand on a slight rise, which has burst from the flat valley like a castle in the sky.

Petroglyphs show that there were early inhabitants in the area. Scientists have examined the rat middens in the huge rocks piled up by nature, and have found plant life thousands of years old by radio carbon dating. Samples include juniper seeds hauled in by rats more than 11,000 years ago. Mr. Willis died in 1925, and Mildred abandoned her dream, moving to San Diego.

The Haddans spent thirty years on the ranch, driving to Barstow or to Lucerne Valley for supplies with one break. In 1946, Albert W. Harris, a wealthy Chicago businessman, established an Arabian horse ranch in Chino. He persuaded Buck to move to Chino and operate the ranch. Esther and Buck lived on the ranch. Buck traveled to the Haddan Ranch to check on his own animals as often as possible. Esther remained in Chino because the ranch there could not be left untended.

Mr. Harris was an officer — and eventually president — of the Arabian Horse Club of America, and was reported to have virtually held the club together. He also wrote and published books.

After two years of being confined to the Chino Ranch, and hard-put to keep their own place going, the Haddans returned to Ord Mountain. For years books on various subjects continued to arrive from Albert Harris.

Buck's health began to fail in 1974, and they disposed of the cattle. Buck's horse, Franklin D., was also showing signs of slowing down. When Franklin D. could barely get around, Buck asked a friend to shoot the poor animal. Three days later, Buck died at the ranch house.

Esther moved to town. While she and a friend were loading the last of her belongings onto a truck, the house burst into flames and burned to the ground. It is not certain what started the fire. Esther now lives with a view of the south side of Ord Mountain, with her mementos, photos, and books.

Esther still drives to the home ranch for a visit. A corral and a shed, which Buck built, are still in use. While there, she feels as though she has never left the ranch.

**HADDAN RANCH, NEAR ORD MOUNTAIN, WHERE
BUCK AND ESTHER LIVED FOR MORE THAN 30 YEARS.**

SLASH X RANCH

Dave Fisher is a young fellow who operates his cattle ranches in the old and proven ways. The only difference is the truck replaces the wagon. He runs cattle at the Black Ranch, at Ord Mountain, on what was once the Haddan Ranch, and Rattlesnake Canyon, where Heart Bar cattle once grazed.

He runs cattle under the Shield F brand.

In the past year, Dave has encountered a vestige of the old west that he would have been glad to skip. Rustlers were stealing and killing his cattle. In the tradition of the experienced cattleman, Dave tracked the rustlers. He followed tire tracks to a house where with binoculars he observed a man dressing a heifer. Sheriff's deputies arrested the suspects the same day. The case is still in the courts.

Fisher lives on the Slash X Ranch, which is owned by Lee Berry, and lies north of Lucerne Valley. "Ol' Sour-do" Berry says the life of the cowboy was a hard one. But to hear him tell it, he enjoyed every minute. And tell it he does, with enthusiasm and energy. At 85, he still enjoys life — "past and present " — on the ranch. Ol' Sour-do recently underwent surgery for a brain tumor, and even that did not slow him down. He still plays the fiddle and sings dozens of songs he has written. No true blue stuff; Lee tells stories in song based on his experiences, and even finds rhymes for words like "reservation."

As a young cowboy, Lee loved to go to dances, where he fiddled and sang and danced. The long ride home on his horse at daylight was no hardship. Then he had time to think about each girl he had held in his arms, savoring every moment. Life was good. Life was always good.

To Lee, hardship is not negative. It is just something that requires a little time to turn into something positive.

Lee was born in Chelsa, Oklahoma in 1901, the oldest of five children. His grandfather came from Ireland as a stowaway. In 1905, Lee's father filed on land in New Mexico, and the family moved to Texico, where his father went into business hauling freight with a dray wagon.

But Uncle Azz Thomason came on a visit from Arizona in 1909. Mrs. Berry was not well, and it was decided that Arizona might be better for her health. Grandpa and Grandma Crume lived in Springerville, Arizona. Plans were made for the move. There were only three Berry children at that time.

Uncle Azz was an old-timer, and Indian fighter, and he knew the country. He drove Lee's mother and the two younger children to Springerville. Lee and his father stayed in Texico until the ranch was sold, and Uncle Azz returned.

Lee recalls every moment of that trip in a new Studebaker covered wagon with overjets on the sides for beds. Water barrels were lashed at the back. Lee has a similar wagon at his ranch, and he points out that it is not too long or the back would drag, and not too heavy for a team to pull uphill and out of gullies. The top is light enough to be removed so the bed can be used for hauling lumber and other large items when not in use for human transportation. The wagon carried some grain for the horses, but it was impossible to carry hay in those pre-baler days.

Uncle Azz could travel three times faster than the wagon, and he often rode ahead to locate grass and water.

There were tight places and they got into some of the darndest predicaments, Lee remembers. But Uncle Azz rode a good strong saddle horse which could be used to help the team pull the wagon out of a bad spot.

Arizona was not yet a state, and was sparsely populated. The travelers came across many small ranches run by Mexican families. They were glad to have visitors, and urged them to stay on. The Mexicans were hospitable and curious, anxious to know all about the strangers. The children were courteous and entertained the visitors with song and dance. Occasionally they came to habitation with a store. The storekeeper knew the territory for fifty miles around him, and could direct them to grass and water.

When the horses grew "gant," grass and water had to be found, even if it meant going in the wrong direction. The party would stop and camp until the horses were in good shape, sometimes staying a week. Enjoyable days, Lee said.

After a particularly heavy rain, the wagon mired in mud. There was nothing to do but to lay over until the ground dried out. It was a good place with plenty of grass for the horses.

They set up camp. In the morning, a visitor arrived — a beautiful white mule. It was an old mule, because its ears came together at the tips, so old it could have been black when young, Lee said. A US brand on its neck indicated it was an Army mule, possibly a veteran which had encountered Pancho Villa in Mexico. It was gentle and obviously glad to see them. A terrible scar ran down one side where the ribs had been cut.

The sun was bright. The travelers opened their bedrolls and spread them to air. Uncle Azz spread out the hide of a mountain lion he had killed. The hide was beautifully tanned, and still had the head attached. The gentle old mule astonished everyone by attacking the bedroll and trashing the hide. "He pawed that mountain lion all to pieces and wrecked the bed," Lee said. The mule was taking revenge for an attack by a mountain lion, they concluded.

The remains of the hide were stowed away, and the mule followed the wagon the rest of the way. Near the end of the trip, the Berrys met a tracker with a tired old horse. He was very glad to acquire the mule. "I never saw that old mule again," Lee said mournfully.

Lee's dad was fond of pinion nuts, and bought them at every opportunity. He looked forward to reaching pinion country.

One night the group made camp after dark, under a huge tree. A pinion tree. Seventh heaven. They hobbled the horses, cooked the meal, and settled down for the night. Dad cracked pinion nuts, and cracked, and cracked. But the nuts had been frozen and were rotten, he said. A big disappointment. In the morning they awoke at daylight to find they were camped on sheep-grazing land. No pinion nuts. "Well, it was funny at the time," Lee said.

But eventually they reached pinion country, and discovered a wonderful way to harvest pinion nuts. All across the country they had seen nests of small twigs, some up to four feet high and four feet wide. They were rats' nests. The rats made an entrance some distance from the nest, and dug up into the center, which they lined with grass. Here they stored pinion nuts. One nest might contain three or four gallons of cleaned and polished nuts. Dad finally had his fill.

Lee remembers crossing the New Mexico-Arizona border near Springerville. Northeast of Springerville was a high mesa which ended in a cliff where a road had been dynamited to allow descent into Round Valley. "To the south was the most beautiful mountain I've ever seen," Lee said. Escudilla Mountain. It was Geronimo country. There was an Indian superstition connected to the valley, and the Indians never bothered the white men who camped there. When this became known, it did not take long for the valley to become completely settled.

At Springerville they were greeted by the family. After a few days' rest, preparations were made for the whole family to move on to Phoenix where Dad hoped to get work on the All-American Canal. Uncle Azz agreed to guide them across the mountains to Phoenix. There were few roads. The nearest town was Cooley.

Lee was anxious to reach Cooley. For many days he had been hearing about Mr. Cooley, who had been raised by the Apaches, and for an unknown reason, his nose had been cut off. Lee was anxious to see this phenomenon. And he did. Mr. Cooley was a nice gentleman, a successful rancher with several Indian wives. And only part of his nose was missing. The town has since been renamed McNary.

The travelers moved on. Eventually they reached Phoenix, and Dad worked on the canal. Lee's sister Ione Jones has written a small book on their childhood and school days. Lee left home when he was sixteen years old, and worked as a cowboy in New Mexico, Arizona, and eventually California.

Lee and his wife Mary still host trail rides from Slash X. But he is not partial to the old days. The Slash X Cafe welcomes bikers, truckers, campers, and tourists. Lee enjoys showing visitors mementos from his cowboy days, including photos, a well-used forge, a sourdough pot, and a gate with no hinges which is set in a sourdough pan covered with cowhide to keep the sand out. And he'll still fiddle and sing songs about girls and cattle and girls and cowboys and girls and Slash X.

OLD CORRAL ON THE HADDAN RANCH.

MCHANEY CATTLE BRAND

CATTLE BRANDS

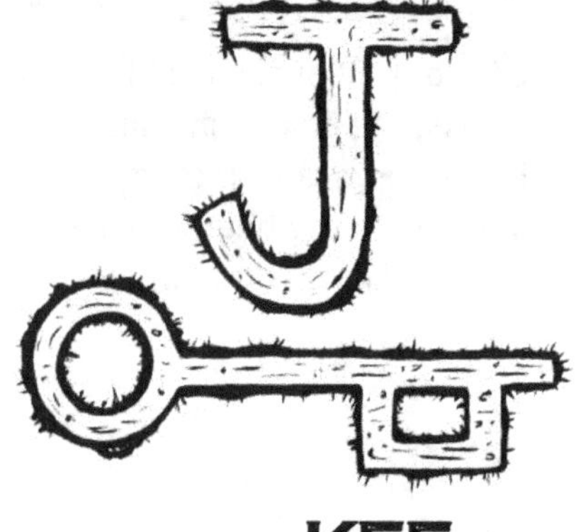

KEE

MCKINNEY

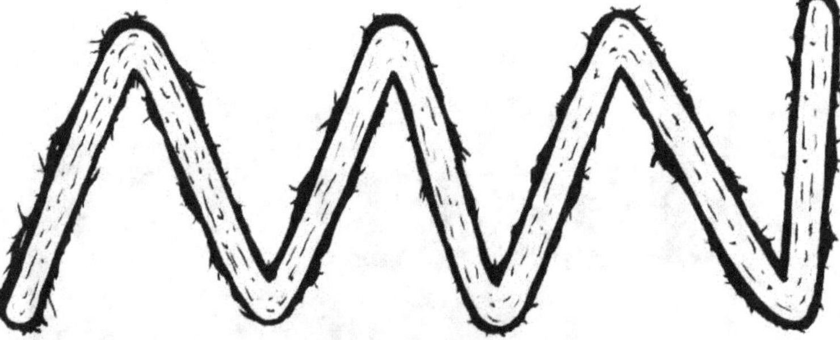

WARREN

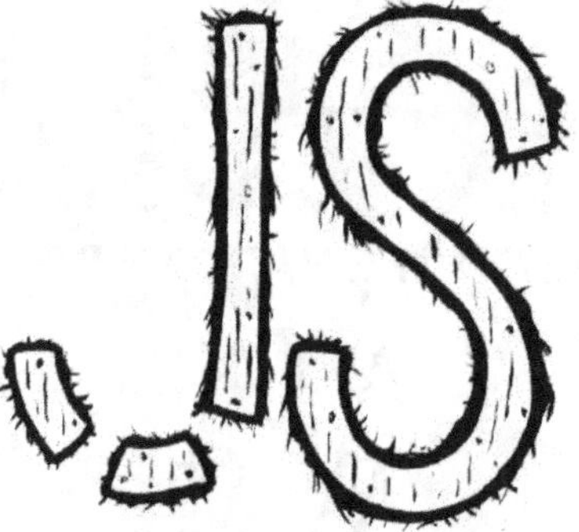

TALMADGE

RYAN

SMITH

KENDALL STONE

Kendall Stone knows the cattle empires of yesterday, the cowboys and cattlemen, the horses, the ranches, ranges, water holes, and trails. His record of history is appearing in the Big Bear and Yucca Valley newspapers and will soon be published in book form.

Stone was born into a cattle family, the Talmadge Brothers. His great grandfather was Frances Lebaron Talmadge, Indian fighter, drover, and buffalo hunter, who established a sawmill in the San Bernardino Mountains. The Talmadge and Caley Sawmill near Arrowhead was water-powered. It was moved to what is now Blue Jay, where it was powered by a one-lunger donkey engine.

The three Talmadge brothers, Will, John, and Frank, were raised in the area and were involved in the mill and lumbering. Stone's grandfather was John, the middle son, "Peg" to his contemporaries and "Puppup" to his grandchildren.

One of the teamsters who worked at the mill was Charlie Martin, a good friend of Puppup's, Stone remembered.

The Talmadge ox brand was the ampersand (&) reversed, which later became Jim Stocker's horse brand. The Talmadge Brothers established the IS Ranch. Their cattle ranged over 750,000 acres of the ranch and leased government land.

Stone first came to Yucca Valley in 1925 with his grandfather to help gather cattle for the spring roundup and drive to Big Bear. Yucca Valley was then known as Warren's Well. From Yucca Valley the cattle were driven across Johnson Valley and into Rattlesnake Canyon, the same route used by Swarthout. Once in a great while IS and Heart Bar herds might be moving at the same time. Just below Rose Mine, the cattle were driven through the Needle's Eye, where the trail divided. The IS cattle went up the Golden Stairs, and Heart Bar on to Round Valley.

Stone remembers Albert Swarthout as a small man with a high IQ, who ran a tough outfit. Swarty and Charlie Reche developed the water at Old Woman Springs. They thought up, figured out, and dug by hand the well that resulted in 150 miner's inches of water, an accomplishment admired in later years by hydraulic engineers.

Nothing phased Swarty. In rough country, where no chuckwagon could move, Swarty loaded bedrolls, beef and beans on burros and herded his cattle over rocks, through canyons and brush. Many of the burros, now living in the San Bernardino Mountains, are descendants of Heart Bar animals.

Heart Bar cattle were wild, skitterish, and crafty, but were controlled by competent cowboys like Charlie Reche, Clay Lewis and Howard Whipple. "They were tough rough-country wild-cattle hot-desert and cold-mountain cowboys," Stone said. He recalled watching in amazement as Howard showed what he could do on a good Heart Bar horse.

Heart Bar and IS men were out after a small bunch of wild cattle in Upper Antelope. Puppup roped a cow, but its calf ran down a brushy, rocky canyon with Kendall and Howard in pursuit. The calf took off at a hundred miles per hour down the steep side of a rocky hill, where it was impossible for a horse to walk. Kendall's horse went down in a pile of rocks and scrub oak limbs. Howard went down the hill covering three hundred yards in five seconds. Speed, momentum and ability carried him to the middle of the rock pile, where he roped the calf, dismounted, and tied the calf down. It took Howard ten minutes to lead his horse from the spot where he had arrived going full tilt.

Stone credits Howard, the horse, and Swarty for the accomplishment. Swarty bred and raised some of the best horses ever seen in the San Bernardino Mountains, Stone said. He brought in American saddlebred studs to breed with his mares, and the result was a wise, sure-footed, desert-smart animal.

But Howard was "some kind of a brave hombre" to get it all together and make it work. It was the challenge that made the cowboy work for $30 a month, Stone says. A cowboy's joy was to track and find a smart cow that knew how to hide in rough country, an animal that could run like a horse, and often outwit its pursuers.

The rancher and the cowboy did not always see eye to eye, but the combination worked. The cowboy was born to chase cattle. The rancher was running a business. An owner would prefer that a wily, elusive cow be left in the brush and rounded up later in open country when it calmed down. Time and effort could be put to better use than risking horse and man. It is well known that the cowboy also liked to live it up and show off when he went to town.

Stone was in the middle. He rode with the cowboys and understood them. But being a member of the family, he knew the rancher's side. So he walked carefully to avoid doing anything that could embarrass the Talmadge family. Stone says the life of the cowboy was the most interesting, exciting and challenging way of life ever envisioned. "And, sadly, a thing of the past."

He defends the cattlemen, and tries to straighten out popular misconceptions. The ranchers never overgrazed or damaged the land as some would like to believe. On the contrary, cattlemen developed water and fought erosion. They started new grasses and browse. "One cow for two grasses, not two cows for one grass" was the motto. Cattlemen developed roads, created private game preserves, and donated land for public animal refuges. The range was the cattleman's livelihood, and he maintained it as best he could.

Stone also deplores the tendency to immortalize the bad apples as cowboys who robbed and killed for no reason. The real cowboy was a tough, hard-riding man who rode eight to twelve hours a day. His prey was a knowledgeable old steer that knew every trail and every rock, tree or bush that he could hide behind. A wise old animal could hear a cowboy whisper or rustle a bush, and be gone instantly. Cowboys found enough adventure tracking, roping, branding, driving without going outside of the law.

Stone has great respect for Swarty and his ability to run an efficient operation. He also surmises that much credit should go to Mrs. Swarthout as a partner in the business. Mrs. Swarthout always went full tilt. Stone remembers eating with the ranch hands at Old Woman Springs when Mrs. Swarthout did the cooking. She was a small woman who trotted between stove and table almost at a run. Her diary indicates she was always busy cooking, canning, raising chickens and turkeys, and feeding a constant stream of visitors.

Stone recalls an unsubstantiated story that sometime before the ranch house was built at Old Woman Springs, Mr. and Mrs. Swarthout spent a winter at what is now the Smart Ranch in the mountains south of Old Woman Springs. They supposedly lived in a cave dug into a hillside, and evidence of such a cave is still visible. True or not, Stone believes it is an indication of the kind of hardship the Swarthouts would endure if necessary.

Stone has had plenty of experience with which he can compare and evaluate the life of the cowboy. He has served in the San Bernardino Sheriff's Department for forty-five years, for ten years as undersheriff, and although retired, is still on call.

During World War II, he was in the First Special Service Force. The FSSF was dubbed the "Devil's Brigade" by the Germans, and has been immortalized in book and film. According to history, the men fought in the cruellest of terrain against murderous opposition. "They were equalled by few and surpassed by none." The brigade was a combined force of Canadian and American soldiers, and although reputed to be misfits, some were and some were not. But all had fantastic skill and endurance. The story of scaling Mont La Difensa may be unequalled.

Stone has returned to the land where he grew up: to his ranch, his horses, and his wife Mary, a horsewoman of note. And he is reliving the old days by writing it all down and setting the record straight.

MAURICE DONAHUE

On the north side of Johnson Valley there is an empty space once filled by Donahue: pioneer painter, raconteur. Maurice did not fit him, so he was always called Donahue.

Donahue came to Johnson Valley in the twenties to prove up on land for a relative. Vague memory says a sister had filed on the land. Donahue lived in a two-room shack without benefit of amenities. His bathing facility was a tub in the open air, heated by the sun long before hot tubs were chic. He enjoyed his freedom and he painted. He had a system. Fastening a mirror to a wall, he painted from the reflection. The mirror focused his subject.

He had another system. He did not wash sheets. He allowed them to quietly expire, and purchased new ones. One day he felt rich, and bought a beautiful shiny white washing machine. Later on a friend saw him in town, buying sheets as usual, and inquired as to the health of the new washer. It was fine, he said. But it was so clean and pretty he could not bear to soil it with dirty linen. So it stood, admired, untouched, pristine.

Donahue got around. He had a truck. One day he returned to his ranch with a ladyfriend in his oxidized gray Ford pickup. The two friends enjoyed the happy hour. When the sun sank slowly into the western horizon, Donahue lit a kerosene lamp. In due time bugs were attracted to the light. They swarmed in and speckled the ceiling. The ladyfriend attempted to kill the bugs, one at a time, all of them — with a pistol. The ceiling was well-ventilated. Fortunately, Donahue was not.

Donahue was a cheerful fellow. He enjoyed life. He became a "character." He was welcome in the homes that sprang up in the valley. His reputation spread.

A visitor to the desert asked to meet him. She was driven out to Donahue's by a friend. As they approached the house, Donahue emerged from his tub under the windmill. The driver stopped the car and attempted to distract the lady from what would be a most embarrassing situation. (This was long before cable TV.) Shielding her view, he tried to explain the delay and the problem.

"Where? Where?" she cried, shoving him aside. "Let me get my good eye on him."

People gave things to Donahue. Furniture. Household items. He never scorned these gifts. That would not have been polite. So he stored things in the second room until it was stacked so high, so full he could not get in there, and was forced to live in one room. Donahue's paintings are still around, hanging on the walls in many homes in the valley. Like many other Johnson Valley pioneers, Donahue was worth getting your good eye on, and one of our beloved historical treasures.

OIL PAINTINGS BY JOHNSON VALLEY ARTIST MAURICE A. DONAHUE
-DONATED BY STAN AND DIXIE COUTANT TO THE MORONGO BASIN HISTORICAL SOCIETY

STONE MEAT HOUSE & RANCH HOUSE AT OLD WOMAN SPRINGS.

BUNK HOUSE AT OLD WOMAN SPRINGS.

THE SHEHORN RANCH

When Woodrow Shehorn was in high school, he promised himself that someday he would have a ranch with a white house, a white fence, white horses, white cattle, and a white dog.

He kept his promise, although the dog is brown, the fence is wire, and the cattle were just plain old cattle colors. No matter. The ranch is a beautiful sight as one comes down the hill from the west and looks over Johnson Valley.

Lois and Woody were early settlers, arriving in 1946. Woody was a successful building contractor in Glendale, with a wife, three children, and a nice home when he announced he was ready for the great adventure — to become a farmer. Lois made the proper wifely sounds — screams of horror at leaving civilization. But chauvinism prevailed, and Woody jumped into his Willys pickup and headed for Humboldt County. There he found rain, moss, mud flats and a strong odor of fish. He returned to Glendale.

A few days later he hopped onto his motorcycle and headed inland, away from wet, fishy smells. At Cottonwood Springs he encountered a herd of cattle swarming over desert and road. Woody made loud motorcycle noises until a small path was cleared, through which he plunged. Down the hill he came, and was rewarded with the sight of paradise. A beautiful, clean, empty valley spreading out below, blue sky above, fresh desert smells.

At Old Woman Springs he called on the residents, Mr. and Mrs. Albert Swarthout, and was told the James place was for sale on the north side of the valley. On-site exploration revealed there was a shack, a well, a windmill and a tree. Woody contacted Mr. James in Victorville, and terms were discussed.

Woody returned home. In his mind the tree grew and flourished, and alfalfa covered the valley. He drove Lois out to see paradise. The tree seemed to have shrunk, the shack had grown smaller, and there was no alfalfa. Back home Woody pondered for two weeks.

Then action! Back to Victorville where, at three a.m., he awakened Mr. James who answered the knock in his long underwear, puzzled at the urgency. Sagaciously James remembered expenses incurred in the two-week interval, and upped the price $700. But the deal was made.

Back in Glendale, Woody conned Lois into accepting the deal by bribing her with a new Packard convertible coupe so that she could visit friends and family in Glendale whenever she wished.

The Shehorns moved to the ranch. Woody put a new roof on the shack and added wallboard to the interior. He planted alfalfa. There were few residents in the area. The Swarthouts at Old Woman Springs. Donahue was nearby. Jerry Willis, his mother Daisy Crawford, and her mother lived on the south side. That was about it. A few families had spent brief sojourns in the valley, but found it was too far from town.

The first big wind arrived one January night. The family was roused by l00-mile-per-hour gales hurling rocks against the house. Chunks of wallboard were blown off, providing an open picture window of blowing sand. Woody and Lois nailed new boards on. Fast!

They began enlarging the house, and bought a herd of cattle. Twenty head, all bred. The first effort was unsuccessful as Woody was not experienced in midwifery or the necessity for it in cattle raising.

Lois enjoyed her travels in the Packard. One day it rained. The fabric top was soaked. The sun emerged and beamed warmly, splitting the top down the middle. Time for a change. They sold the Packard and bought a Jeep, 3-disc harrow and a Ford woody station wagon in telephone company green. Woody scraped and varnished the wagon to a beautiful shiny gloss. Lois used it for grocery shopping in Victorville, taking the three children with her, the youngest still a baby. One day while driving home, she reached into the glove compartment for oatmeal for the baby. The car left the road and flipped over; A road crew working a quarter-mile away saw the accident and rushed to the scene. No one was hurt. The men righted the car and Lois drove home.

It was Woody's turn to make horrified noises at the sight of his once shiny wagon.

The cattle business did not prosper partly due to the arrival of homesteaders, and partly due to inexperience. Woody went to work down below, coming home as often as possible. He built the house into a substantial home with a walled courtyard, a huge fireplace, thick walls, plenty of bookshelves, and all the amenities. The original shack is the existing kitchen, back porch and basement. The children had horses to ride, and swam in the reservoir.

The children are grown and Woody has retired. An airstrip has been built south of the house. Pioneering! It sounds easy, but it wasn't. It just sounds that way when Woody tells a story in his inimitable upbeat style, which is as good a way as any, and better than some.

OLD WOMAN SPRINGS IN 1928.

OLD WOMAN SPRINGS IN 1998.　　-FROM THE BILL WILSON COLLECTION

CHANGES

Johnson Valley is full of movers and shakers who have made the community a great place to live. Among the early arrivals were Agnes and Gust Valentine. Their son Eric was one of the first to apply for a homestead with a deposit of $10 in 1954. The Valentines joined forces, paid the rest of the fee, and received a map with numbers. The desert spread out before them. Somewhere out there was their five acres. The only people near them were Daisy Crawford and her son Jerry Willis, who had filed on 640 acres in 1947.

Gust called a surveyor, and on returning to the desert some weeks later found yellow stakes marking their five acres. He also found a couple working on the frame of a cabin nearby. The Camps were the first to build on a five-acre homestead, Gust said. By that time many others had filed.

Being a busy contractor in Pasadena, Gust and his son did not get around to building their cabins right away. It was April, 1956 when the two cabins were finished. By then there were many others in the valley, and a feeling of community began to grow.

Plans evolved for an improvement association and for a community building. Ina Goodridge and Daisy Crawford scurried around the desert signing up people as members of the association.

Rummage sales were held down on the highway. Gust remembered many a trip trucking rummage down to the site. There was quite a gang involved, he said, rattling off names like Nelson, Means, Alders, Smith, Lafon, Cathey, Jarvis, Breese, Ballard, Norton, and Estes.

A building did go up. In 1967 the Valentines made a permanent move to their cabin and began to participate more earnestly in the growth of the association. One of the first projects was to finish the stonework by the front entrance. Agnes and Gust helped an Italian named Burt sift sand, mix cement in a wheelbarrow, and gather stones from the area. Karl Swenson painted the building.

But it bothered Gust that toilet facilities consisted of an outhouse with braces to keep it from falling down. And what of the possibility of a snake surprising an unwary visitor? With the help of building chairman Alex Chernoff, toilets were built. Gust painted the outside and stained the inside.

Gust had the building fever. He couldn't stop there. There had to be a kitchen. Jim Cathey and Jack Waller decided that members could build it themselves. Gust couldn't wait to get started, and the Valentines bought the first load of lumber. The foundation was poured, and Clarence Estes was official water boy to keep it wet and prevent cracking.

Gust made a drawing of the kitchen, showing the rafters and walls. The cost was estimated, and members were given the opportunity to buy a specific amount of building materials. Names were inscribed on the drawing, showing what each person donated in the way of rafters, plywood, roofing paper or two-by-fours. A thermometer showed the progress of the building fund.

Howard Kidd, Jack Waller, and Clarence Goodridge did much of the construction with help from association members. The women kept busy bringing food for the workers. Many a potluck was held to raise funds. The Nowickis, Hazards, Owens and Warrens were among the helpers, Gust recalled. But Gust was sure of one thing. He was the first registered voter in the valley, and the event was recorded by the Yucca Valley Newspaper. The clipping was on the wall in the association hall until it disappeared.

The organization, which began as the Grandview Improvement Association, is now the Johnson Valley Improvement Association. Gust is gone, as are many of those mentioned here, including Daisy Crawford, Clarence Estes, Jerry Willis, Rocky Nelson, Bob Hazard, and Dan and Eva Jarvis. The association is still growing. Members are still busy working, and a church is under construction as the valley continues to prosper.

PHOTO GALLERY &

STUDIO PHOTOS OF AL SWARTHOUT AS A YOUNG MAN AND AL & LILLIE'S OLDEST CHILD, HELENE SWARTHOUT, AT EIGHTEEN MONTHS.
-BOTH STUDIO PHOTOS FROM THE KELLEY COLLECTION

UPPER END OF OLD WOMAN SPRINGS ALFALFA FIELD LOOKING WEST.

ADDITIONAL MATERIAL

LOU WESCOTT BECK, SHOWN HERE DRIVING HIS 1912 FLANDERS ALONG WITH HIS DOG RUFUS, ERECTED SIGNS TO DESERT WATER SOURCES. THE SIGN READS "OLD WOMAN SPRINGS 17M."
-FROM THE HAROLD & LUCILE WEIGHT COLLECTION

VIRGINIA CREEPER SUN SHADE AT WALTER RECHE'S HOMESTEAD.

KIT RECHE AND SON MORGAN IN FRONT OF THEIR ADOBE HOMESTEAD. WALTER RECHE BUILT IT WITH 1,320 HANDMADE ADOBE BRICKS.
- LAST 2 PHOTOS ON THIS PAGE FROM THE MORGAN & MIQUE RECHE COLLECTION

ALBERT SWARTHOUT ON ROWDY. ALBERT WAS KNOWN TO BREED FINE HORSES.

BOX S RANCH IN 1896. FIRST HOMESTEAD OF ALBERT R. SWARTHOUT.

SURPRISE SPRINGS - WALTER RECHE ON THE LEFT.
-FROM THE MORGAN & MIQUE RECHE COLLECTION

CABIN AT AMES WELL. DONALD SWARTHOUT ON THE LEFT.

**MYNARD SWARTHOUT, AGE 4 OR 5, 1933 OR 1934, ON FORDSON
TRACTOR AT OLD WOMAN SPRINGS.**

THE HOMESTEAD WHERE MRS. MCNANY WAS HIT ON THE HEAD AND KILLED BY A PLANK THAT BLEW OFF THE CHICKEN COOP DURING THE NIGHT OF THE BIG WIND, JANUARY 27TH, 1916.

MESQUITE WELL - ONE OF THE MANY WATERING HOLES FOR THE HEART BAR CATTLE.

A ROCK CORRAL SINGLE-HANDEDLY BUILT BY MILDRED WILLIS.

ESTHER HADDAN BY ONE OF MILDRED WILLIS' MANY ROCK WALLS.

MILDRED MOVED AN ESTIMATED 1,372,000 POUNDS OF STONE TO BUILD WALLS, CORRALS & TROUGHS LIKE THE ONE PICTURED BELOW.

WALTER RECHE (RIGHT) AT BIG MEADOWS, HEART BAR RANCH.
-FROM THE MORGAN & MIQUE RECHE COLLECTION

HOMESTEADER'S SHACK THAT CHARLIE MARTIN MOVED TO MOUND SPRINGS AFTER HIS STOVE WAS STOLEN BY A HOMESTEADER.

**THE PINEAPPLE EXPRESS ON THE COTTONWOOD AND SOUTHERN
RAILROAD AT OLD WOMAN SPRINGS RANCH.**
-FROM THE BERT & DONNA BARBER COLLECTION

A VIEW OF OLD WOMAN SPRINGS FACING NORTH.
-FROM THE BERT & DONNA BARBER COLLECTION

WED 50 YEARS—Mr. and Mrs. Albert R. Swarthout of 2340 G street are shown cutting their golden anniversary wedding cake at their home where a reception was held to mark the event.

Swarthouts, Pioneer Residents, Honored on Golden Wedding Day

Golden wedding anniversary of Mr. and Mrs. Albert R. Swarthout, members of a widely known pioneer family, was observed at a reception at their home at 2340 G street.

Scores of relatives and friends formed the company that participated in the observance and watched Mrs. Swarthout cut the anniversary wedding cake.

During the year three Swarthout brothers, all native sons of San Bernardino celebrated their golden wedding anniversaries. The other brothers are George E. Swarthout now of Hermosa Beach, and Charles P. Swarthout now of Valley, Wash.

The three brothers are the sons of the late George W. Swarthout. The elder Swarthout was a pioneer of 1847 and the family name has been stamped on this region for nearly a hundred years.

Assisting Mr. and Mrs. Swarthout at the reception were their son and daughter, Mr. and Mrs. Donald M. Swarthout of Altadena. Their three grandchildren, My-

nard, Elizabeth and Janet, were also present.

Mr. and Mrs. George E. Swarthout and their daughters and children were here for the occasion. Various other members of the family residing in San Bernardino were present.

Mrs. Ida Hauhuth of Vallejo, Mrs. Swarthout's sister, made the trip south for the reception. Mrs. Hauhuth, Mrs. Charity S. Kelley, Mrs. J. M. Guest and Mrs. Fred W. Schwalm poured at the tea table. Mrs. Jeanette Phillips of Hollywood was here for the occasion.

Paul Shoup of Los Angeles, a school mate of Mr. Swarthout in the early days of San Bernardino, sent his greetings.

Mr. and Mrs. Swarthout were married Feb. 10, 1895 at Alhambra, the home of Mrs. Swarthout's parents. They left yesterday for their desert ranch home at Old Woman Springs.

Coffee sold for $3 a cup in Richmond, Va., at the close of the Civil war.

FROM THE SUNDAY, FEBRUARY 14TH, 1945 EDITION OF THE SAN BERNARDINO SUN.

LEFT TO RIGHT ARE DALE GENTRY, ALBERT SWARTHOUT AND NORA KELLEY GUEST, SWARTHOUT'S NIECE. THE TWO FORMER PARTNERS MET FOR THE LAST TIME AT HEART BAR RANCH, BIG MEADOWS, IN MAY, 1963, JUST SIX MONTHS BEFORE SWARTHOUT'S DEATH AT THE AGE OF 91. THE STATE ACQUIRED THE RANCH IN 1964 TO TURN INTO A PARK & CAMPGROUND. ALL OF THE ORIGINAL BUILDINGS WERE DEMOLISHED. -BOTH PHOTOS FROM THE KELLEY COLLECTION

WATER TOWER, TICKET OFFICE AND ENGINE HOUSE FOR GENTRY'S PINEAPPLE EXPRESS.

GENTRY'S HOUSE AT OLD WOMAN SPRINGS RANCH.

OLD WOMAN SPRINGS RANCH IS PRIVATE PROPERTY & IS CLOSED TO THE PUBLIC.

STONE MEATHOUSE AND SWARTHOUT RANCH HOUSE.

BARN AT THE RANCH IN 1998.

-ALL FOUR PICTURES FROM THE BILL WILSON COLLECTION, 1998

BARKER & SHAY COWBOYS IN THE EARLY 1900S.
- FROM THE JIM BAGLEY COLLECTION

CATTLE CAN STILL BE SEEN GRAZING THROUGH BURNS CANYON
TODAY. -PHOTO BY DIDIER CHEVALIER

DETAILS OF HEARTBAR RANCH PURCHASE IN 1921. THIS WAS ONE OF THE DOCUMENTS USED AS EVIDENCE IN THE LITIGATION BETWEEN SWARTHOUT & GENTRY ON HOW THE RANCH WAS TO BE DIVIDED.

1921		Cattle Stock	Cash of Ranch	-	1921
April 11 Purchased from the					35,000.00
Dr Blair estate, cattle estimated at			1922 Cash of steers (feeder)		7,171.00
					42,171.00
600	head - stock cattle				
91	Bull Calves Branded				
88	Heifer " "				
779					
250	Feeder Steers purchased				
1029 Total 81 Twos - 169 Yearlings					

Jan
15-1922

Cattle on hand........................…..... 1029

	H	B	
May 25	36	28.................	64
June 10	15	15.................	30
July 3	19	12.................	31
" 14	8	4.................	12
Sept 5	7	7.................	14
Oct - 24	18	9.................	27
	1	2.................	3
Dec 8	8	7.................	15
" 30	8	2.................	10
	120	86	

PAGE FROM ALBERT SWARTHOUT CHECK REGISTER DURING 1936.

Checks by Swarthout

1936		
	Bal. Fwd -	$53.23
Sept 28	Safe Way -	5.60 ✓
Oct. 3	Safe Way -	4.89 ✓
„ 7	A. L. Corman Truck repair	14.40 ✓
„ 7	Gilmore Oil Co.	13.50 ✓
„ 7	Ind. Feed -	7.05 ✓
„ 7	Safe Way -	5.82 ✓
„ 17	A.J. Burlow. 19 gal gas. 2 oil	5.14 ✓
„ 14	Safe Way -	3.66 ✓
„ 21	J.R. Bruehman (Hay)	14.00 ✓
„ 21	Safe Way -	2.45 ✓
„ 30	„ „ (Joe acct)	39.10 ✓
„ 30	A.L. Corman Truck.	14.52 ✓

A PAGE FROM LILLIE'S DIARY - AUGUST OF 1946 - WHILE LIVING AT OLD WOMAN SPRINGS

Aug 46		Aug 46	
10	Janet & I picked	14	Dad took old ice box
	peaches, cleaned		to Randel, got ice
	hens nests - some		etc -
	thunder, no rain	15	Ice box O.K. cement
11	Mr James here		work O.K.
	visited quite a while		filled tank - irrigated
	Company		picked fruit
12	Janet & I got big	16	Dad irrigated - to Victor
	box handy for ice		got chicken feed, mail
	fed horse		Postman walked in, ice
	Dad here from	17	Dad irrigated, picked
	Mts - hard trip		apples, shot birds, fixed
	here late P.M.		pipe -
13	Dad worked on box	18	Dad irrigated - had
	for cooler all day		lot of company
	fixed cement for		
	(unreadable) Pipe		

DONALD M. SWARTHOUT
3046 CLARMEYA LANE
PASADENA, CALIFORNIA 91107

May 24, 74.

Dear Bill:
I was really pleased to hear about you from Pappy Giles and chatting over the phone brought back old times. I had asked about you several times at the club but the information all added up to zero which made me wonder if your back had really laid you low. And now for a few notes about Old Woman Springs and Johnson Valley.

My father, Albert R. Swarthout, (Al.) bought a half interest in the Heart Bar ♡ cattle ranch in late 1906 or 1907. His partner was Charley Martin. (Charley) Charley had used his homestead rights at Glen Martin, now Camp Angelus in the San Bernardino Mts. So father arranged to file a homestead on Old Woman Springs. At that time two men, Yeager and Lord had each filed homesteads at Old Woman but were squabbling over the water. Dad bought them both off and filed one homestead for himself and another was filed for "Slim" Purdue. Both homesteads were completed and dad bought Purdue's property. Correction — The partnership of Martin and Swarthout bought the Homesteads. They made Old Woman Springs the winter headquarters for the winter cattle range. Water was developed at the mouth of Rattlesnake Canyon. Two holes, One hole (west of Longhorn canyon, (now Bighorn) . . . . at Cottonwood Spring.

Handwritten letter written by Donald Swarthout to Bill Guldborg in May 24, 1974

DONALD M. SWARTOUT
PASADENA, CALIFORNIA 91107

Dear Bill:

I was really pleased to hear about you from Pappy Giles and chatting over the phone brought back old times. I had asked about you several times at the club but the information all added up to zero which made me wonder if your back has really laid you low. And now for a few notes about Old Woman Springs and Johnson Valley.

My father, Albert R. Swarthout, (Al) bought a half interest in the Heart Bar ♡ cattle ranch in late 1906 or 1907. His partner was Charley Martin (Charley). Charley had used his homestead rights at Glen Martin, now Camp Angelus in the San Bernardino Mts. So father arranged to file a homestead on Old Woman Springs. At that time two men, Yeager and Lord had each filed homesteads at Old Woman but were squabbling over the water. Dad bought them both off and filed one homestead for himself and another was filed for "Slim" Purdue. Both homesteads were completed and dad bought Purdue's property. Correction—The partnership of Martin and Swarthout bought the homestead. They made Old Woman Springs the winter headquarters for the winter cattle range. Water was developed at the mouth of Rattlesnake Canyon, Two holes, One hole (West of Longhorn Canyon, (now Bighorn) Rock Corral, Quail Springs and at Cottonwood Springs – owned in fee. They bought 40 acres and placed the 40 acres to include Cottonwood Springs.

Soon after Old Woman Springs was underway, the Government opened up that area for homesteading. Nearly all the land was filed upon but very few homesteads were proven. That was around 1908-1912-14. For many and sundry reasons all the settlers moved out. Poor soil, wind, too far from market or just plain discouragement.

After World War II, more homesteaders came in and the present Homesite Act populated the area.

About 1910-or 11 father and Charley stayed in the small shack at Rock Corral, during the winter, and developed the water found in two springs approximately ¾ of a mile S. and E. of the corral. They had purchased 4 miles of 2" pipe from a bankrupt mining company for $100.00 and used a part of that pipe to bring the water to the corral. The Rock Corral was built by a man by the name of Swett.

In 1914 Charley Martin sold his half interest to Dr. E. Scott Blair of San Bernardino. In 1919 father sold to Bob Bryant and in 1920 Dr. Blair bought out Bob Bryant. Dr. Blair, his wife and only son were hit by a passenger train at Hesperia and all were killed. In the settlement of Dr. Blairs estate father and J. Dale Gentry bought the entire ranch. This was in 1921.

Father developed the water at Mesquite, (hand dug and also drilled well) windmill and a 2700 gal. tank. Well and wind mill at Mean's. Strong winds took down 2 mills so then he scraped a trench to water which was about 16' deep. I believe that area is now set aside as a water reserve. Nearly forgot-the 40-acre piece of land at Mesquite Well will be set aside for public use. They also developed water at Ames and stone reservoir and troughs. Then 4 miles south of Ames another well, windmill + tank called the "New Well" for lack of a better name.

We all knew Charley Reche, his wife and family very well. Sons Warren and Walter, and daughter Margaret. For many years Charley helped with the cattle during the Spring roundup on the desert, driving to the mountain range, then the beef drive, the fall roundup, and from the mountains to the winter range on the desert again. From Charley Reche we got the straight of the part that he played in the Willie Boy hunt. The author of the book, Lawton, has done a very good job of getting the story as Charley told it to him and to us.

Guess I'd better quit,

        Sincerely

        Don

P.S. Really glad to know you are feeling better. If in this area give us a ring-you might catch me home.

A PAGE FROM ALBERT SWARTHOUT'S DIARY WHILE WORKING AS A RANGER FOR THE FOREST SERVICE.

	Sept 05		Sept 05
Sund 10	Left home at 8 A.M.	**Thurs 14**	Left home at 7:30 on trail
	on trail past 7 Oak's		through Barton Flats to
	to Clark's ranch home		mouth of South Fork and
	same way at 4:30. 14 mi		up to Sugar Loaf (unreadable)
Mond 11	Left home at 7:30 A.M.		Home at 5 P.M. 18 mi.
	on trail to Glen Martin	**Frid 15**	Left home at 8 A.M. on road
	home same way at 5 P.M.		to the Clarks and then on
	18 mi. Met Ranger Allen on		to Lower Barton through
	Seven Oaks Trail		the Dry Cienega
Tues 12	Left home at 8 A.M. on		Home by Jenk's Cabin
	trail past Balls ranch up		at 4 P.M. 14 mi.
	Fossee Creek to Jenks Lake	**Sat 16**	Left home at 8 A.M. on
	home at 5 P.M., 16 mi.		road to Clark's ranch home
Wed 13	Left home at 7 A.M. on		same way at 4 P.M. 16 mi.
	road to Clark's ranch home by	**Sund 17**	Left home at 7:30 on road to
	Snyder's ranch at 4:00 P.M. Saw		Big Meadows. Home same
	smoke of fire over toward N. Creek		way at 5 P.M. 20 mi.
	and phoned to Redlands. They	**Mond 18**	Left home at 7 A.M. on trail
	said it was over at Richie Canyon		to (unreadable) Bear Valley
	near (unreadable) home at 7 P,M. 20 mi		(unreadable)

BURROS AT THE HEART BAR RANCH

Donald M. Swarthout, in his article in Outdoor California November-December 1975 "The Other Side of the Burro," writes that "burros were a part of the working force, along with cowboys and horses, on our Heart Bar Cattle Ranch in San Bernardino County for more than 45 years." They possessed unique qualities that made them suitable for ranch life and work in the Mojave Desert. They have excellent feet, can travel farther from water to better grazing and have less water requirements than other animals. They are strong, tough, surefooted and methodical and possess keen eyesight and hearing.

They are masters at conserving energy and can flourish in conditions that kill other animals. In 1922 and 1923 a severe drought occurred in the Mojave Desert winter range. Cattle losses amounted to 65 percent and horses nearly 50 percent. On the other hand, there were virtually no burro losses.

Burros were especially useful on the Heart Bar Ranch during the 75-mile 3-day cattle drives twice a year between the desert area around Old Woman Springs Ranch and the summer pastures at Big Meadows in the San Bernardino Mountains. They were almost indispensable. They packed grub, bed rolls, pots, pans and feed. They were "ideal for this job, since they traveled slowly and stayed with the herd." When approaching camp for the night, they would leave the drive and wait at the trail shack to be unpacked.

Tough guy Charlie Martin, Albert Swarthout's first partner at the Heart Bar Ranch, may have had the highest regard for burros of anyone. His ride of choice was a burro named "Grover Cleveland."

Eventually, burros and even horses to some extent were replaced by the Ford Model T and then the first pick-up trucks – the Ford Model TT first appeared in 1917. This accounts for the sudden surge in the feral burro population when prospectors released and abandoned no-longer-needed burros and converted to mechanized travel. Visitors to certain areas of the Mojave Desert even today encounter their descendants wandering around either by themselves or in herds.

ITINERANT PROSPECTOR MR. GILLUM & HIS WORKING BURROS.

A BRIEF HISTORY OF THE COTTONWOOD & SOUTHERN RAILROAD

In 1958 J. Dale Gentry indulged his passion for railroading by bringing a locomotive, caboose and two flat cars to Old Woman Springs Ranch where he installed three miles of narrow-gauge track. The locomotive, one of the last steam engines in Hawaii, and other cars had been used on a Hawaiian sugar plantation prior to being acquired by Gentry. He named his little track and locomotive the Cottonwood and Southern Railroad – but it is better known by its nickname, the "Pineapple Express."

Gentry was more than just a railroad buff. As a young man he had worked as a fireman for the Southern Pacific Railroad in Arizona. Later he worked for a small logging railroad hauling timber for the Brookings Lumber & Box Company. While living in San Bernardino, he would sometimes appear at the local Santa Fe Railroad yards and ask if he could run the engines.

Every year on his birthday, Gentry brought two busloads of his friends to Old Woman Springs and treated them to rides on his "shortline" railroad. In 1966, he took his train to the National Orange Show held in San Bernardino. Despite its popularity and Gentry's efforts to make the train a permanent attraction, there were at least three collisions with automobiles during the show & officials did not invite Gentry to return the following year.

Dale Gentry died in 1974 in San Bernardino and in 1976 the division of his $3.5 million estate was finalized. Old Woman Springs Ranch was put up for sale at $325,000. The train, including the Baldwin Saddle Tank .062 locomotive, two flat cars, three railroad cars, the water tank and its supporting structure, all the track, and as many as 6,000 railroad ties was sold for its appraised price of $43,500. The Beverly Hills investor who purchased the train intended to ship it to the Santa Cruz area, possibly Roaring Camp in California's "Gold Country", and keep it operating.

ESTATE OF J. DALE GENTRY STILL UNSETTLED: By Leonard Metz

Sun-Telegram Staff Writer: Monday, March 22, 1976

OLD WOMAN SPRINGS RANCH – The little locomotive stands silent. It has been sold to a Beverly Hills railroad buff and will be moving north within the next few months.

The big three-acre lake is still. No one fishes for the bass, bluegill and catfish stocked there and no one walks the beach of the smaller lake nearby.

The guest house is quiet. So is the 2,049-square-foot main residence. No one has lived there since its owner, J. Dale Gentry, died May 20, 1974. Only in the caretaker's house are there sounds of human occupancy.

Old Woman Springs Ranch is still unsold. And until buyers are found for the $325,000 ranch and two other still-unsold parcels, the $3.5 million Gentry estate will remain unsettled.

Nevertheless, large sums of money have already been distributed by the trust department of Bank of America, which is administering the estate.

Two $250,000 trust funds have been set up, a number of $25,000, $10,000 and $5,000 bequests have been paid, and nearly $100,000 apiece has been given the San Bernardino Valley Lighthouse for Blind and Shriner Hospital for Crippled Children in Los Angeles, two organizations that will inherit the bulk of the estate.

Gentry, 90 when he died, was San Bernardino's first Ford dealer. He was a man who believed in keeping his assets largely in cash, and his estate proves it.

He left a savings account containing $1,689,000, and another with $23,093. The safe in his office at the California Hotel contained $6,881 in cash, and there was $17.54 more in nickels and pennies in the office.

There was $16,000 in his checking account, and he had a $65,000 deposit certificate and another for $50,000. He left sacks of gold and silver coins that were sold to the U.S. Silver Corp. for $88,141.

Last May the Bank of America set aside $128,000 to guarantee eventual payment of Gentry's inheritance taxes. He left 228 shares of Bank of America stock and a $445,000 secured loan.

Possibly the smallest item in his estate was a $1.90 refund check for cancellation of his subscription to National Geographic Magazine.

Offered as a package with the 357.48-acre Old Woman Springs Ranch is the 40-acre Cottonwood Springs Ranch a quarter mile east. Gentry owned the properties since the 1920s, when they were used for cattle ranching. He and his partner, A. L. Swarthout, wintered their cattle there, and grazed them at Heart Bar Ranch in the mountains during the hot summer. When Swarthout and Gentry split up, Gentry retained Old Woman Springs and some mountain property and Swarthout acquired control of Heart Bar.

Gentry's mountain property is valued at $300,000. It contains 537 acres three miles north of Barton Flats. There is a cabin on the land, but there is no water and the only access is through a ranger station road.

His third unsold parcel, in the desert near George Air Force Base, containing 20 acres. It is valued at $20,000.

Mrs. Frances Crossland, Bank of America trust officer, said the properties are hard to sell because of "market conditions." Old Woman Springs was maintained by Gentry as an estate and resort, and no one seems willing to pay the $325,000 price to maintain it on that basis, she said.

Gentry had been a railroad worker before starting the Ford Agency in San Bernardino in 1911 and after becoming successful told friends he wanted a railroad of his own.

The locomotive, built in 1897, was discovered on a Hawaii sugar plantation. Gentry bought it in 1957 and shipped it to Old Woman Springs where he built two miles of track, an elevated water tower, an engine house, a depot and a railroad barn.

Each year on his birthday, April 12, Gentry would bring his friends to Old Woman Springs in two buses to celebrate the occasion and ride in the train. In 1966 Gentry brought the train to the National Orange Show where it carried show visitors on a track circling the grounds. However, there were three collisions with automobiles and although no one was injured, show officials rejected Gentry's offer to bring the train back the next year.

Last month the train and most of the train property were sold to George A Cordingly Jr., a Beverly Hills real estate investor, at the appraised value of $43,500. The sale, negotiated by San Bernardino Realtor Sanford J Blau, included the Baldwin Saddle Tank .062 locomotive, two flat cars, three railroad cars, the water tank and its supporting structure, all the track, possibly 6,000 railroad ties, the depot, and other appurtenances.

Cordingly said the train would not be turned into a museum piece, but would be kept running. Although plans are not complete, it seems certain at this time the train will be put to use in the Santa Cruz area, possibly at Roaring Camp, he said.

Crossland said there have been "nibbles" by persons interested in the Old Woman Springs property. It has four natural springs providing 1,500 gallons a minute. At one time, it was used to raise alfalfa.

The Shriners Hospital and Lighthouse for the Blind have each received around $97,000 from the estate and stand to share in the income from more than $2 million eventually she said. This includes about $1.5 million already set aside and an estimated $665,000 when the final three parcels are sold.

Gentry's will, dated Nov. 30, 1972, set up two $250,000 trust funds – one to provide a life income to his two sisters; the other, a life income for Charlotte Arth, a friend during the last 20 years of his life.

Arth was also bequeathed a house at Lake Arrowhead and purchased Gentry's Lincoln Continental from the estate at the appraised price of $5,750.

The trust fund for the two sisters will pass to two nieces when the sisters die. The Arth trust fund will revert to Lighthouse for the Blind & the Shriners Hospital on her death.

Two of Gentry's nephews each received $25,000 outright, and a number of acquaintances including women who knew Gentry 60 years before his death, received $10,000 each.

Gentry was never married and left no children.

My dad and I met Dale Gentry at Cottonwood Springs one afternoon while he was actually at the controls of his locomotive, running it along the rails between there and Old Woman Springs. He saw us, stopped, and we had a pleasant albeit brief chat.

 Mr. Gentry's hired man, Glenn Moritz, was there also, carrying a partially filled five-gallon can of grease in one hand, and a wooden stick with a rag haywired to it in the other. He was greasing the inner edge of the rails where they curved around Cottonwood Springs. My dad and I assumed the locomotive's wheels were binding against the tracks because the curve was a bit tight.

This was the one and only time I met Mr. Gentry.
- Stan Coutant

LOS ANGELES EXAMINER

Automotive	Slim's Pickin's
Motorlogue	From the Pits

SUNDAY, JUNE 14, 1959   PAGE 9, PART E

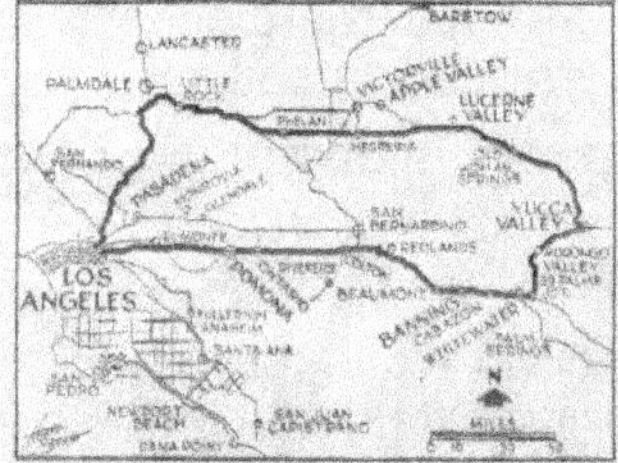

ROUTE of Motorlogue Party to Lucerne Valley.

Motor & Outing

"PUFFER-BILLY," 22-ton Baldwin locomotive built in 1897, pulls flat car and caboose over three-mile track on Dale Gentry's Lucerne Valley ranch. Gentry, once a railway engineer, got train from Hawaii plantation.

RANCHER Dale Gentry handles throttle of his locomotive for quick run over private track on his huge ranch at Old Woman Springs in Lucerne Valley.

Homesteading in Lucerne Valley Offers Many New Way of Life

By SLIM BARNARD
Examiner Automotive Editor

Thousands of people have found a new and relaxed way of life on the Southern California desert, thanks to a Federal law that opened huge areas of public land for small homesteads.

One of the best examples of how the Small Tract Act has benefitted the average person is the Lucerne Valley of San Bernardino County, where five-acre tracts—each with its own house—stretch over rolling country to the mountains on the horizon.

We were amazed by the possibilities for relaxation offered in Lucerne Valley while on a Motorlogue in a 1959 Edsel Villager. This excellent auto showed a lot of power combined with good economy.

Our route to Lucerne Valley was via Highway 99 through Redlands and Beaumont to the Twentynine Palms turnoff, just south of White Water. This road climbs through a fascinating gorge to the communities of Yucca Valley and Morongo Valley.

From Yucca Valley another road leads over the mountains toward Lucerne Valley and Apple Valley, and as soon as you cross the crest the panorama of hundreds of homesites appears.

Although this is desert country and the season is advancing, daytime maximum temperatures at this time of year seldom exceed 90 degrees. However, it is wise to carry extra water on mountain roads.

The 1938 Small Tract Act opened unused public land in desert and mountain areas for residence, recreation or business purposes at varying costs.

These tracts in Lucerne Valley cost a total of $25 for five acres, which includes $10 for filing fees and $15 for lease of the land. The lease price is refundable if the deed is not proved out.

One of the specifications for ownership is a minimum improvement, which in most cases is a 400-square-foot house built for around $600.

Almost every one of the 12 by 16-foot retreats in the valley also is topped by a water tank that can be filled from water trucks for a cent a gallon.

However, we stopped at a more elaborate tract, the Jim-N-E Ranch owned by Mrs. James Mounts, of Glendale. Mrs. Mounts has added a main house and guest unit, for a total of about $4000.

Her house is built on a knoll, and from it we could count 50 other small homesteads. Still, there was plenty of blue sky and big country for everyone.

Continuing to Old Woman Springs—the Western desert is a treasure of colorful place names—we met Dale Gentry, rancher and native of San Bernardino.

Gentry, with expansiveness to match his land, has built a railroad on his ranch—a genuine antique

Turn to Page 11, Cols. 1-2

"SIGNS IN THE DESERT" point to five-acre homestead tracts in Lucerne Valley where thousands of Southland residents have found a delightful new way of life and recreation.

EDSEL VILLAGER, official Motorlogue car, passes through one of Lucerne Valley's five-acre homestead tracts with 400-square-foot, $600 homes. Other homes are in background.

Automotive Motorlogue **Slim's Pickin's** **From the Pits** *Sunday June 14, 1959*

Motor & Outing **Homesteading in Lucerne Valley Offers Many New Way of Life**

By Slim Barnard *Examiner Automotive Editor*

Thousands of people have found a new and relaxed way of life on the Southern California desert thanks to a Federal law that opened huge areas of public land for small homesteads.

One of the best examples of how the Small Tract Act has benefitted the average person is the Lucerne Valley of San Bernardino County, where five-acre tracts---each with its own house---stretch over rolling country to the mountains on the horizon.

We were amazed by the possibilities for relaxation offered in Lucerne Valley while on a Motorlogue in a 1959 Edsel Villager. This excellent auto showed a lot of power combined with good economy.

Our route to Lucerne Valley was via Highway 99 through Redlands and Beaumont to the Twentynine Palms turn off, just south of White Water. This road climbs through a fascinating gorge to the communities of Yucca Valley and Morongo Valley.

From Yucca Valley another road leads over the mountains toward Lucerne Valley and Apple Valley, and as soon as you cross the crest the panorama of hundreds of homesites appears.

Although this is desert country and the season is advancing, daytime maximum temperatures at this time of year seldom exceed 90 degrees. However, it is wise to carry extra water on mountain roads.

The 1938 Small Tract Act opened unused public land in desert and mountain areas for residence, recreation or business purposes at varying costs.

These tracts in Lucerne Valley cost a total of $25 for five acres which includes $10 for filing fees and $15 for lease of the land. The lease price is refundable if the deed is not proved out.

One of the specifications for ownership is a minimum improvement, which in most cases is a 400-square-foot house built for around $600.

Almost every one of the 12 by 16-foot retreats in the valley also is topped by a water tank that can be filled from water trucks for a cent a gallon.

However, we stopped at a more elaborate tract, the Jim-N-E Ranch owned by Mrs. James Mounts, of Glendale. Mrs. Mounts has added a main house and guest unit, for a total of about $4,000.

Her house was built on a knoll, and from it we could count 50 other small homesteads. Still, there was plenty of blue sky and a big country for everyone.

Continuing to Old Woman Springs — the Western desert is a treasure of colorful place names — we met Dale Gentry, rancher and native of San Bernardino.

Gentry, with expansiveness to match his land, has built a railroad on his ranch---a genuine antique steam locomotive with cars and a caboose that runs over three miles of track.

Actually, the train was what attracted us to Gentry's ranch, for we almost believed it to be a mirage of the desert. However, Gentry proved it was a real "puffer-billy," the result of a long-time dream.

Engineer

As a youth Gentry worked as a railrway engineer in the Yuma area, but he had visions of owning his own railroad. Instead, other things got in the way, and he ended as a hotel owner and rancher.

Recently, though, he was the guest of the owner of a large Hawaiian Islands plantation, and there he found the 22-ton Baldwin locomotive.

The steamer, built in 1897, still was in good condition, so Gentry shipped it, rails and all, to his Southern California ranch.

Now, dressed in engineer's costume, with a red bandanna around his neck, and at the throttle of his locomotive, Gentry looks to be a far cry from the gentleman rancher and hotelman that he is.

Return Trip

After a very pleasant visit with Gentry, we started the return trip via Hesperia.

This proved to be quite a contrast, for where the Lucerne Valley is dotted with $600 weekend cabins, Hesperia has residences in the $15,000 to $50,000 class. Yet in both places the residents are enjoying unsurpassed quiet and climate.

Following the trip home via Cajon Pass and San Bernardino, we visited the Bureau of Land Management office at 215 West Seventh street, where applications under the Small Tract Act are received.

Nolan F. Keil, manager, told us the Lucerne Valley section is closed to applicants right now, as is the rest of San Bernardino, San Diego and Kern counties, due to a backlog of 15,000 would-be homesteaders.

Other Land

However, there is still land available in other areas, and besides, grants that have not been proved up are sold by auction or at drawings conducted by the bureau.

Whether you are looking for a place away from it all or merely a nice desert trip, we can recommend the Lucerne Valley jaunt. There are several good motels in Yucca Valley, Joshua Tree or Hesperia.

BRANDS

The San Bernardino County Recorder was responsible for examining burned imprints from the branding irons brought in by livestock owners. They then recorded them in the *San Bernardino County Brand Book*.

While most of the imprints submitted to the county were made on small square sections of leather, some cattlemen brought in brands upon anything that they had available — such as wood or recycled leather strips taken from old furniture or luggage.

The following pages contain examples of the many different cattle brands filed in the San Bernardino County Museum's Historical Archives.

THE HEART BAR LEATHER CATTLE BRAND .

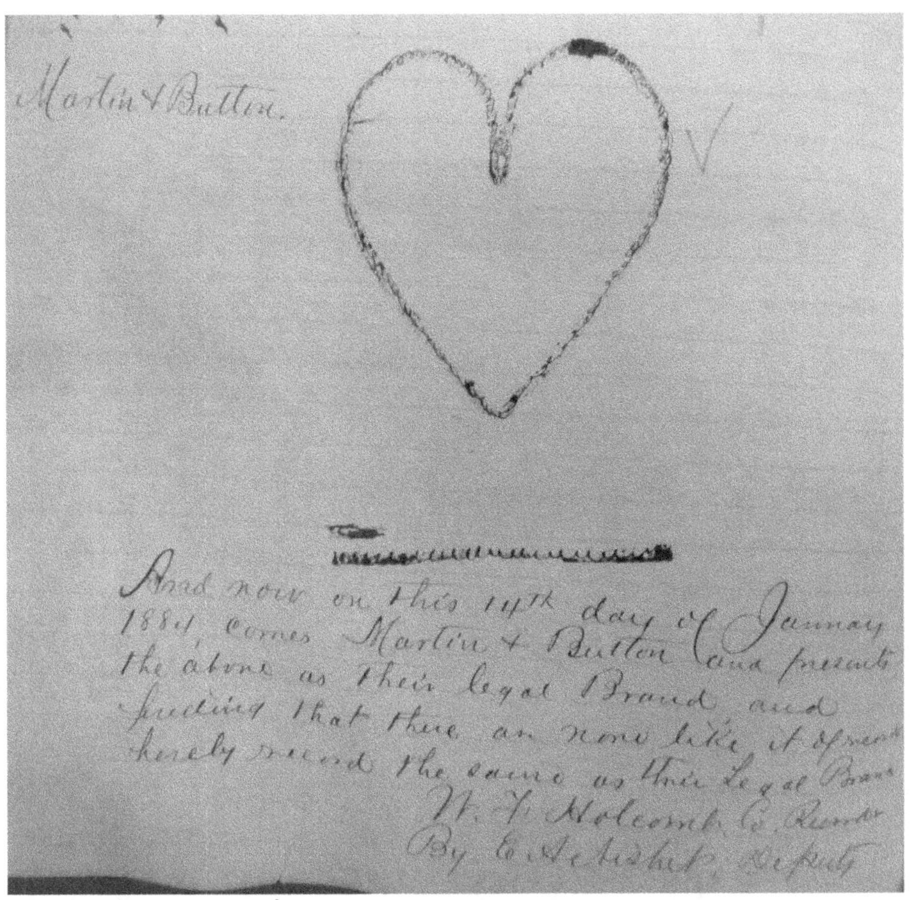

And now on this 14th day of January 1884, comes Martin + Button and presents the above as their legal brand and finding that there are none like it recorded hereby record the brand as their legal brand.

W. F. Holcomb   Co. Recorder
By E A Nisbet   Deputy

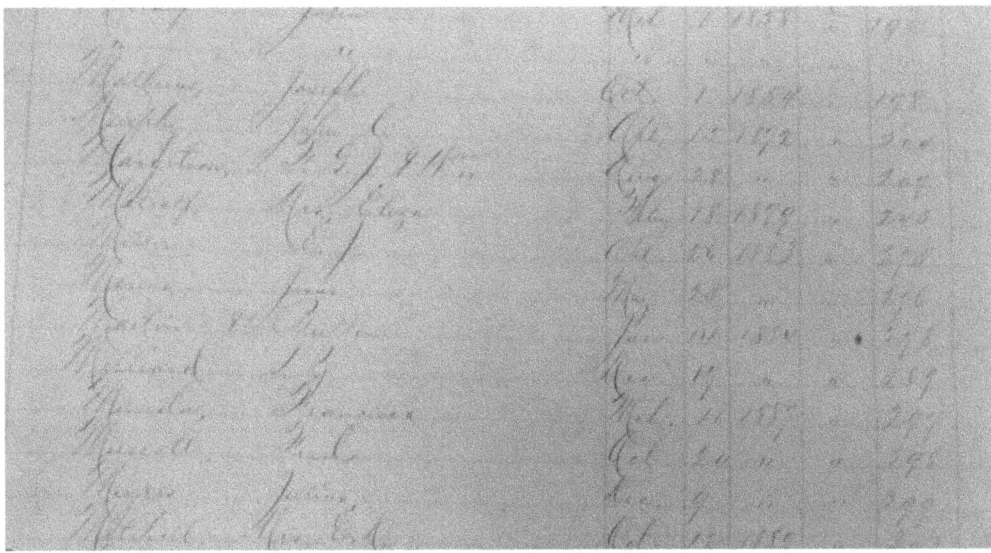

THE 1884 HEART BAR RANCH BRAND IS RECORDED ON THE LEDGER ABOVE. MARTIN & BUTTON'S RECORDING IS THE 7TH ENTRY.

MARK WARREN'S (WARREN'S WELL) LEATHER CATTLE BRAND.

JOHN C. CARTER'S LEATHER CATTLE BRAND RECORDED ON WOOD.

J. F. HOUGHTON - JANUARY 14TH, 1878.

FRANCISCO MUNDA - MARCH 11TH, 1887.

VICTOR C. SMITH - JUNE 12TH, 1911.

E. M. SMITH - JANUARY 29TH, 1889.

ALFRED HEAP - MAY 5TH, 1890.

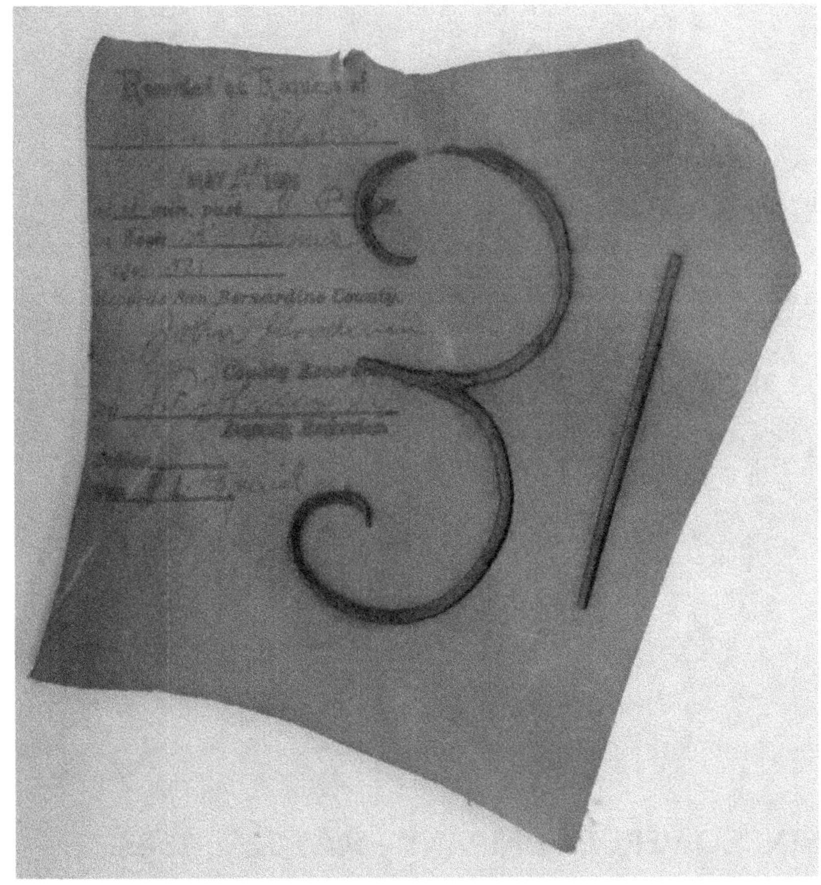

JOSEPH E. WILSHIRE - MAY 11TH, 1893.

J. S. LORD - DECEMBER 13TH, 1893.

RANCHO VERDE COMPANY - MAY 12TH, 1903.

H. C. BLANCHETT - OCTOBER 7TH, 1915.

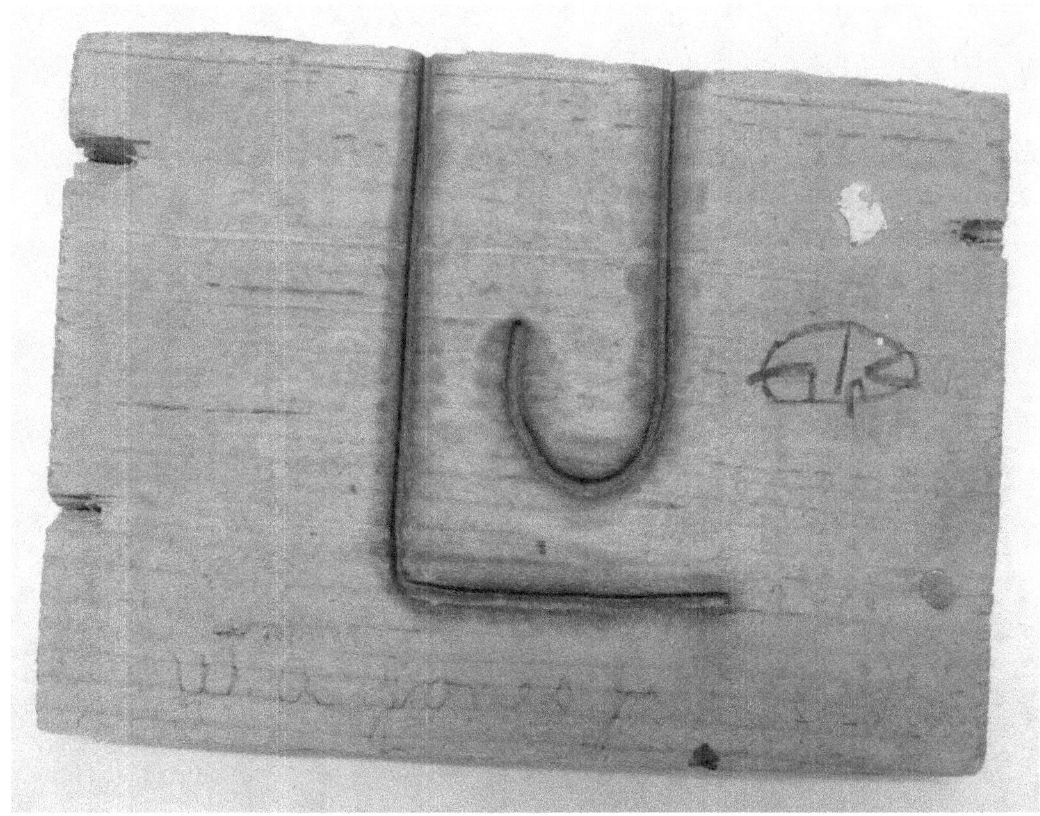

W.A. JONES - FEBRUARY 15TH, 1916.

JOHN SPITLER - NOVEMBER 7TH, 1854.

J. M. ANTHONY - JUNE 4TH 1907.

JAMES SINGLETON - DECEMBER 1ST, 1878.

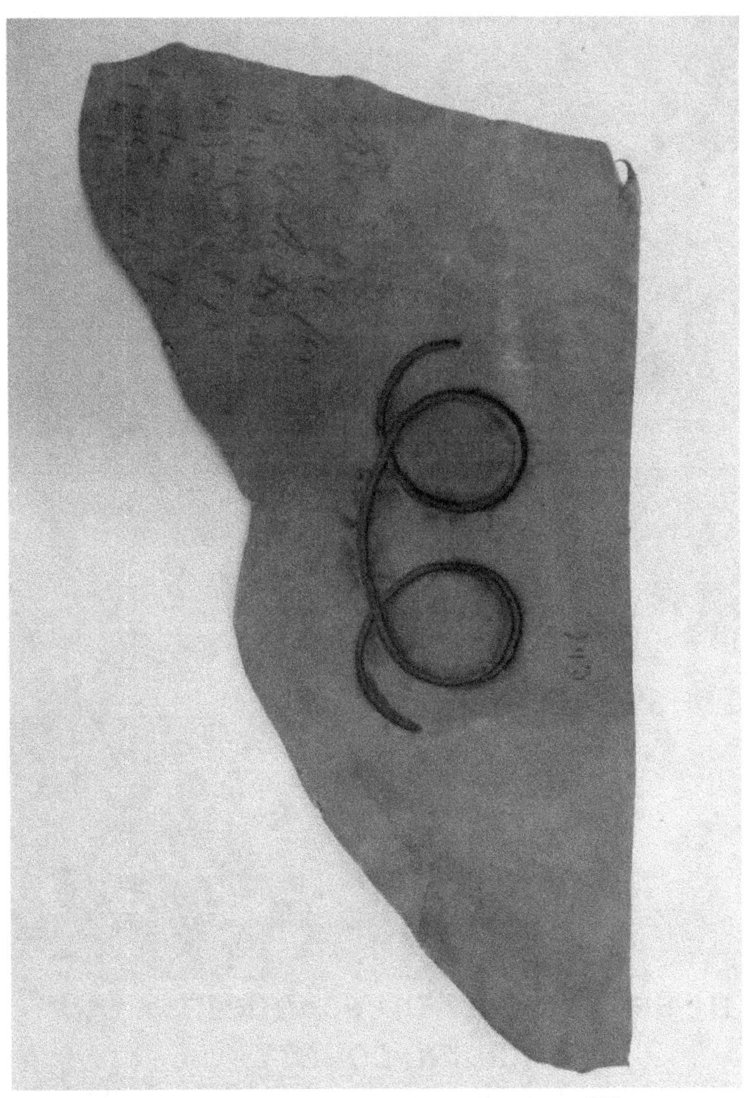

JOHN SUVERKRUP - NOVEMBER 16TH, 1878.

CATTLE BRANDING IS STILL PRACTICED IN SAN BERNARDINO COUNTY.

-PHOTOS IN THIS COLLAGE WERE TAKEN BY HILARY SLOANE, PHOTOJOURNALIST.

SOURCES

1. Barnard, Slim "Homesteading in Lucerne Valley Offers Many New Way of Life," *Los Angeles Examiner*, June 14,1959
2. County of San Bernardino Historical Archives, San Bernardino County Museum. 2024 Orange Tree Ln, Redlands, CA 92374
3. Hanson, Steve, "Ames Well Site Report," Morongo Basin Historical Society, May, 2015.
4. Metz, Leonard, "Estate of J. Dale Gentry Still Unsettled," *San Bernardino Sun-Telegram*, March 22, 1976.
5. Metz, Leonard, "J. Dale Gentry Dies at 90," *San Bernardino Sun*, May 21, 1974.
6. San Bernardino Public Library, Arda Haenszel California Room of the Norman F. Feldheym Central Library. 555 West 6th Street, San Bernardino, CA 92410
7. "Pioneer Dies," *San Bernardino Sun*, November 11, 1963.
8. Swarthout, Donald M, "The Other Side of the Burro," *Outdoor California,* November-December, 1975.
9. Lucille Weight Collection, "Photograph of Lou Wescott Beck at Old Woman Springs mileage sign," Mojave Desert Archives, Goffs, CA.
10. Weight, Lucille, "Cattle Brands of the Joshua Tree National Monument Region and San Gorgonio Pass," published by the Joshua Tree Natural History Association, 1975.
11. Wilson, Bill, "When Locomotives Had Names," November, 2008.

MARTHA AND HER SON, STAN, STANDING ON THE SLAB OF THEIR JOHNSON VALLEY HOMESTEAD WITH THEIR 1948 STUDEBAKER COMMANDER IN THE BACKGROUND.
-STAN COUTANT, "OUR VERY OWN JOHNSON VALLEY"

MARTHA AT THE 2004 DEDICATION OF A PLAQUE COMMEMORATING THE HISTORY OF HEART BAR RANCH AT OLD WOMAN SPRINGS.

ABOUT THE AUTHOR

Second eldest of six girls, Martha Wood was born January 20, 1913 in Arlington, Massachusetts. 1924 saw the family move to Pasadena, California where she attended John Marshall Junior High School, Pasadena High School, and Pasadena Junior College. Martha met her future husband Stanley Coutant in Pasadena, and the two were married in 1934 at the Calvary Baptist Church. They lived in Rancho Santa Fe until 1938, when they moved to Sierra Madre.

Son Stanley was born in 1943, and once he started school Martha became involved in the PTA, and was a member of the local board for several years. She wrote numerous works of fiction for magazines including Highlights for Children and McCall's. Eventually she put her writing skills to work as a reporter for the Pasadena Star-News, and later for the Monrovia Daily News-Post as its Arcadia correspondent. Her journalistic career lasted for nineteen years.

During 1958 she began research on what became twelve historical documentaries, the first being *Heart Bar Ranch and Johnson Valley Neighbors*.

Martha was an early adopter of computers, graduating from her Smith Corona typewriter to a Mac in 1986. She continued to embrace technology until her death in 2013 at the age of one hundred.

MORONGO BASIN
HISTORICAL SOCIETY

MORONGO BASIN HISTORICAL SOCIETY

MISSION STATEMENT

The mission of Morongo Basin Historical Society is to collect, conserve and exhibit artifacts; to collect, display and interpret and publish memorabilia relating to the history of the Morongo Basin; to locate, identify and preserve historic sites; to promote the research and study of local history; and to share the rich heritage of the Morongo Basin with all the communities within and surrounding it.

On February 20, 1999 the Morongo Basin Historical Society became an incorporated non-profit entity. The museum and research center located on 2 ½ acres at 632 Landers Lane, Landers CA 92285, was the home of Newlin Landers the founder of the town of Landers and his wife Vernette.

Vernette Trosper Landers, an educator, successfully campaigned to establish a rural station of the Yucca Valley post office in Landers. It was housed in a 400 square foot homestead cabin. Vernette financed and operated the post office herself from 1962 until 1998. The original post office was subsequently moved to the Landers' property where it serves as an exhibit space.

Cattle ranches like the Heart Bar Ranch operation in *Heart Bar Ranch and Johnson Valley Neighbors* by Martha Wood Coutant played an important role in our local history. The first cattle drive through the Morongo Basin in the eastern Mojave Desert was most likely led by Paulino Weaver, the first white man to cross through the high desert, sometime in the 1850's. Driving cattle was a seasonal occupation. Cowboys took the cattle to fatten in San Bernardino mountain pastures around Big Bear for the spring and summer then drove them to the desert ranges for the fall and winter.

Reliable water sources were critical to ranching. Warren's Well in present day Yucca Valley, was one of the most well-known and important in the whole region. It was hand dug by early rancher Mark "Chuck" Warren and his sons. The Morongo Basin Historical Society chose Warren's Well as its official logo. Old Woman Springs, winter headquarters for the Heart Bar Ranch, was another prominent water site.

Open range with space for grazing was necessary to fatten the cattle for market. Cattle ranching peaked in the Morongo Basin in the 1930's. In 1946, large sections of land were subdivided into smaller tracts for homes, businesses and weekend cabins, drastically curtailing open range activity. In 1947 after the last known cattle drive occurred in the area, the cattle ranching era came to an end.

Two historic pioneer families – the Reches and the Warrens – were related by marriage when Charlie Reche married Francis Eleanor Warren, eldest daughter of Chuck and Sylvia Warren. To this day the annual Warren family reunions are attended by hundreds of people from across the country. Chuck Warren and Charlie Reche were among the first to homestead in the Morongo Basin in the Mojave Desert. Charlie Reche and sons Walter and Warren were often employed as cowboys by the Heart Bar Ranch.

The Morongo Basin Historical Society is honored to have cousins Morgan Reche, grandson of Charlie, and Marion Warren Arnett, grandson of Mark "Chuck" Warren, as active members. Their remembrances provide valuable insight into a bygone era of the "Old West" in California.